THE HISTORIAN
AND THE ARMY

THE 1953

BROWN & HALEY LECTURES

*are the first of a series given annually at the
College of Puget Sound, Tacoma, Washington
by a scholar distinguished for his work
in Social Studies or the Humanities
The purpose of these Lectures is to
present an original analysis of
some intellectual problems
confronting the present age*

THE
HISTORIAN
AND
THE
ARMY

Kent Roberts Greenfield

RUTGERS UNIVERSITY PRESS
NEW BRUNSWICK • NEW JERSEY
1954

PREFACE

THIS VOLUME contains the substance of three lectures given at the College of Puget Sound, in Tacoma, Washington, on April 27-30, 1953. They were the first given under the Brown and Haley Lectureship which provides for an annual series of lectures.

My object in preparing these lectures was to invite public attention to certain aspects and results of the most ambitious enterprise in the writing of contemporary history that has been undertaken in our time. This is the history of the United States Army and its Air Forces in World War II, an undertaking which the War Department sponsored in 1945 and which is being completed under the auspices of the Department of the Army and the Department of the Air Force.[1]

This series is of general interest if only as an effort to make official history honest. In what follows I have attempted to review its claim to be honest and illuminating history. I have also invited attention to certain conclusions that its authors are reaching about the way in which we Americans waged our greatest war.

[1] *United States Army in World War II*, K. R. Greenfield, General Editor (Washington: Government Printing Office, 1947—), a series of which 20 out of a projected 96 volumes have been published; *The Army Air Forces in World War II*, edited by W. F. Craven and J. L. Cate (University of Chicago Press, 1948—), of which 5 of a projected 7 have been published.

The material of the lectures was supplied almost entirely by the writings and suggestions of the historians who are writing the history of the Army and Air Forces in World War II. The footnotes will indicate the extent of my indebtedness to them and I gratefully acknowledge that indebtedness. The selection of subjects, which makes no pretense of being inclusive, is my own, and I have suggested certain conclusions for which some of my associates would not be willing to assume responsibility, though to me they seem justified.

I chose the fight at Dornot, in Part II, not because it was important but because it permits me to illustrate, in miniature, the application to battle narrative of the techniques described in Part I. In Part III, I have looked at some of the postwar publications on Allied strategy in the light of findings recorded in the published and unpublished work of our authors on the subject. I am well aware that when their work is further advanced, the slant of light may change, decidedly. In Part IV, in which I felt more at home, having worked in the subject myself, I have reviewed certain radical changes in the shape of our armed forces which appeared during World War II and which have asserted themselves even more decisively since it ended. They seem to me to deserve the attention of every thoughtful citizen.

KENT ROBERTS GREENFIELD

CONTENTS

Preface   *v*

I

An Adventure in Contemporary History   *3*

II

Dornot: Pushing History into the Fog of Battle   *15*

III

Coalition Strategy: The Army's Outlook   *28*

IV

The Army Re-Shaped   *60*

V

Some General Observations   *86*

THE HISTORIAN
AND THE ARMY

I

AN ADVENTURE IN
CONTEMPORARY HISTORY

WITHIN six months after V-J Day the War Department gathered together a group of historians, admitted them to its records, and gave them the task of writing the history of the performance of the War Department, the Army, and the Army Air Forces in World War II. The undertaking was nothing if not ambitious. We were to proceed at once to write the history of almost four years in the life of over 8,000,000 Americans organized for war and engaged in waging it all over the globe. This history was to be comprehensive, including the operations of the whole military establishment, as well as the operations of its field forces. It was, in other words, to be an institutional history of the war as well as a history of campaigns. Another decision regarding its scope was that, although it was to be a history of the Army (I shall use the term "Army" throughout as including both its air and ground forces), it must reach out to include the operations of the Navy and Marines and reach up to include strategic plans and decisions insofar as these conditioned the plans and performance of the Army.

It was decided that this ambitious mission would require the preparation of about a hundred volumes. If a history of such scope and magnitude was to be written and published, it could not be left to private enterprise. It had to be written under the sponsorship and control of the Army. It had to be official history.

This was necessary in order to solve two problems. One was the problem of dollars and cents. The War Department, which recognized its need of having an accurate record of its performance at an early date, was the only institution ready and willing to foot the bill. The other was the problem of giving a large group of historians access to the records of the War Department. This was a poser because a massive proportion of these papers had been subjected to "classification" for reasons of security during the war. The problem of melting down this enormous iceberg of frozen records by a process of review and declassification was insuperable. But all the records of the War Department could be thrown open to historians on its own payroll by simply clearing those authors for access to the most secret records. Clearing for publication the histories they wrote would be a much simpler matter—and has been.

The undertaking that I have sketched is unprecedented in several respects important enough to make it an enterprise of general interest to scholars and the public.

Considered together with the history of Naval Operations being written by Professor S. E. Morison and his staff, the Army's history is unprecedented in being the first sustained effort to produce a systematic history of our military services in war. Before World War I the writing of such history was left to private initiative, which failed to produce it. It has been remarked

that the United States has been one of the most bel-
ligerent but one of the least military of the great nations. This attitude has been reflected in the lack of
serious interest in military history among American
historians. During World War I an ambitious plan for
a history of that war was sponsored by the General
Staff but collapsed shortly after the war when the War
Department failed to sustain it.

Another consideration that makes our enterprise a
matter of general interest derives from the fact that
we are writing contemporary history. The war history
programs of our armed forces, and of the British, rep-
resent the largest attack on the field of contemporary
history that is being made in our time. It is a field into
which historians have been reluctant to push their
scholarship forward on a broad front. Nowadays almost every historian has to write a textbook, and in
his textbook even the most conservative historian has
to write contemporary history, since no publisher will
let him off without a chapter that includes Truman,
Atlee, Stalin, Nehru, Chiang Kai-shek and Malenkov.
In the field of monographs the lid on contemporaneity
blew off long ago if only because of the pressure to
find subjects for the dissertations of innumerable
candidates for the doctor of philosophy degree. But in
the middle zone, between the high, thin generalities of
the textbook and the ground cluttered with unas-
sembled blocks of monographs, historians are still
timid about undertaking projects that look toward the
synthesis of information on major subjects in contemporary history. Ours is such a project.

One reason alone seems to me, as a historian, conclusive for taking the offensive in this field: if we do not do so at once, and on a grand scale, we will lose irretrievably much of the vital evidence needed to answer questions that the future will raise. One would think that the historian had documents enough for the history of World War II. The Army alone produced 17,120 tons of records, enough to fill 188 miles of filing cases set end to end. Nevertheless, one of our main efforts has been to supply the defects and shortcomings of this documentation. Gaps in the written record have been multiplied in our time by the use in war of telephonic and radio communication and of fragmentary or oral orders. More than ever before, many of the most important records are written on air. A prompt and systematic interrogation of surviving participants has been necessary to fill gaps in the written record. On the other hand, the mass of records that has survived is so enormous as to make it increasingly doubtful whether history can be successfully written except by the generation that has created the records and knows how to use them selectively. I am convinced, in short, that unless history is written promptly it cannot be written either correctly or adequately.

Since military history had not been cultivated in this country, either in or out of the Army, when we undertook our history of World War II we had to develop the historians who could write it, and since the intensive study of contemporary history is a relatively uncharted area of scholarship, we have had, in considerable measure, to create our own precedents in that field. Facing these problems we had a great advantage which we exploited. This was the fact that in

World War II the War Department had put many historians in uniform as historical officers, to carry out the President's March 1942 mandate that a record of the Government's administration of the war was to be prepared, and prepared at once. From these historians who had been in uniform we recruited most of our staff. They had learned to know the Army and Air Forces in action, which qualifies them to make military sense of what they are writing. Also they learned by observation how the records they use are generated. They have had, furthermore, an immediacy of interest in what they are writing that has given it realism, and they have a professional interest in giving lasting substance to great events in which they themselves played a part. Under these circumstances we have developed a nucleus of highly competent military historians— something the United States never had before. And these historians have had an experience and acquired a skill in writing contemporary history that would be hard to match.

The most challenging task that faced the professionals in 1946 was to make official history honest. The problem is real and basic. How can any agency of Government avoid issuing self-serving declarations or be expected to clear statements of fact that its officers regard as contrary to their own interest? This may not, indeed, be possible in the long run. But regarding our adventure let me say at once for the Army and Air Forces that if we have not succeeded in putting out honest history it has been our own fault.

We enjoyed a basic advantage in the fact that in World War II the Army wanted a history of its experience in that war for its own guidance, and for this it needed full and frank history. But such history might have been produced for internal use only. The remarkable fact is that we encountered no disposition not to publish what we had written or were to write.

In 1945 *The Infantry Journal* offered to publish the studies that my own historical section had written during the war. I took the matter to General Devers, who was at the time Commanding General of the Army Ground Forces. I explained to him that our studies, then classified "Secret," had been written for internal use and that we had called the shots as we saw them. His answer was: "How is the Army going to progress unless its mistakes are seen and studied?" I warned him that living—and quite powerful—officers might have their feelings hurt. "Well," he shot back, "isn't that the kind of wound a soldier has to take?" I would not mention this incident if we had not found it typical of the Army high command.

General Eisenhower, then Chief of Staff, made this attitude official. When I was offered the position of Chief Historian of the Department of the Army and went to him with the problem of inducing competent professional historians to write under government control, he immediately recognized and took action to meet the conditions that would have to be met if they were to do a professional job. These were three: freedom of access to all records of the War Department necessary to write a comprehensive history; freedom to call the shots as they saw them; and the individual responsibility of the author, signed and sealed by putting his name on his book. This adds up to academic freedom. The only restriction on the contents of our books is that they cannot include information which —to quote one of General Eisenhower's directives to his staff—would *"in fact* endanger the security of the nation." (The italics are his.) That same directive made the exercise of our "academic freedom" not optional but imperative. "The History of World War II," it runs, "must, without reservation, tell the complete story of the Army's participation" [in the war]. "The foregoing directive," he added, "will be interpreted in the most liberal sense with no reservations as to whether or not the evidence of history places the Army in a favorable light."[1]

The proof of the pudding is in the eating. We have had some angry generals on our hands, but have never altered a statement that the historian could document unless the aggrieved party has presented new and reliable evidence to support his criticism. The serious reviewers of our books have testified, with some surprise, but without exception, to our success, to date, in making official history honest. The Army can well take pride in the expression which General Lestien recently used in a review of our series, when he wrote in the *Revue d'histoire de la deuxième guerre mondiale* that the American Army's history has the character of an "examen de conscience."[2]

One final condition had to be met before we could

[1] *Eisenhower Speaks,* edited by R. L. Treuenfels (New York, 1948), pp. 264-65.
[2] General Lestien, "L'Armée Américaine au combat," *Revue d'histoire de la deuxième guerre mondiale,* No. 9, January 1953, pp. 38ff.

write our history. We had to know what the enemy was doing. Lack of this knowledge has in previous wars indefinitely delayed the writing of conclusive history until it could no longer be contemporary. We have that knowledge as an unintended by-product of the much debated policy of unconditional surrender. This put all of our enemies' records at our disposal. We have rounded out this documentary evidence, as we have our own, by extensive and systematic interrogation. As a result we have learned promptly as much about "the other side of the hill" as it will ever be possible to know.

Given all these advantages and the mountains of records at our disposal, the question still remains whether the record available to us is complete enough and accurate enough to permit us to expose the nature of war as Americans fought it in 1942-45.

We can write its institutional history, with reasonable hope of success. But in military history, as in war, "the battle is the pay-off." What about the battle? As one of my historians has put the question: "Is the Tolstoyan view of warfare, that the confusion of battle is so great and the din of battle so loud that no commander, let alone a historian writing [never so soon] after the event, can give a true picture of what was going on?" Have we succeeded any better than our forebears in penetrating "the fog of battle"?

To get the testimony of participants and get it as soon as possible is one method of doing this. We pushed this method hard during the war, and we have exploited it diligently since, in reference to all the subjects of our endeavor.

S. L. A. Marshall, military editor of the *Detroit News,* long a student of war, and in 1944-45 Chief of the Historical Section of the European Theater of Operations, first applied the method on a large scale to the 7th Division on Kwajalein in 1944. He conducted mass interrogations of groups of soldiers when they came out of battle.[3] The results convinced the commanders of the inadequacy of the Army's battle reports as evidence of what had happened in battle. Marshall's mass interviews were inapplicable in Europe, but the interrogation of survivors was extended to all theaters. The Army organized teams of historical officers who were sent to the scene of every action they could reach that seemed likely to be decisive. They interviewed survivors, studied the terrain, and collected fugitive records. The pay-off of the method appears in our *American Forces in Action* series, fourteen volumes devoted to small-unit actions, as well as in the battle pictures in our big history. Of the *Omaha Beachhead* volume in *American Forces in Action* a veteran wounded on that cruel beachhead wrote us: "It is the only book or treasure I have of my own experiences and it is positively an accurate description of events, which surprises me." I like to believe that the *Saturday Review of Literature* was right when it characterized our small-unit narratives as ". . . the most exact descriptions of battle ever written."

As I have said, we continued to apply the method of interviewing the participants after the war and have applied it to all the subjects of our research. We have

[3] See his *Island Victory* (Washington, 1944), Chapter I, "How the Truth of Battle is Found."

amply demonstrated its value as a technique that could and should be applied much more widely to research in recent history. But it yields diminishing returns as time passes. Even the most honest memory quickly fades and becomes distorted. "On the actual day of battle naked truths may be picked up for the asking; by the following morning they have already begun to get into their uniforms."[4] As our recent Chief of Military History, Major General Orlando Ward, liked to put the matter: "Hindsight, tricks of memory, and new information lend reason to happenstance."

But, valuable as they are, interviews are only a supplementary resource. Accurate and detailed exposition of battle action still depends on written records and the skill and imagination with which the historian uses them. The experience of our historians to date has led us to the conclusion that the inadequacy of military records is often exaggerated and that an alert and well-trained historian can make these records, checked and supplemented by interviews, yield the picture that the Army and the public so eagerly desire. Let me restate this conclusion in the words of Dr. Philip A. Crowl, whose name is on two of our forthcoming combat volumes.[5] "After action reports are often defective or unreliable. But, we have a basic record in the journal that every Army unit in action keeps. This is the equivalent of a ship's log. In its

[4] Sir Ian Hamilton, *A Staff Officer's Scrap-book during the Russo-Japanese War* (5th impr., London, 1907), p. v, quoted in Teggart, *Theory of History* (New York, 1921), p. 22.

[5] Philip A. Crowl and Edmund G. Love, *Seizure of the Gilberts and Marshalls;* Philip A. Crowl, *Campaign in the Marianas,* forthcoming volumes in *United States Army in World War II.*

rough form, it is kept by an enlisted man, and if properly maintained is a minute by minute recording of all
radio and telephone messages that come into or go out
of the command headquarters. The man who writes
these entries is strictly neutral. He neither knows nor
cares enough about plans, tactics, etc., to be able in-
telligently to distort the record. True, his superior
officer may come along later and erase a message or
lose a sheet of the journal, but any such tampering
with the record would go hard on the tamperer if dis-
covered. Army regulations as well as custom, tradition,
and fear of discovery would normally militate against
it.

"These journal entries are of course often erroneous
because of mistakes made either at the sending or re-
ceiving ends. Company commanders report their loca-
tions incorrectly, give mistaken impressions of the size
and composition of the enemy they are facing, etc.
Some, in fact many of these errors, can be corrected or
eliminated by the orthodox historian's device of check-
ing the eyewitnesses against each other. The journal
of one unit must be checked against those of adjacent
units, and if the Navy is operating in the area, against
ships' logs and naval action reports. The American
accounts must be checked against whatever enemy records are available. Finally, the interviews conducted
on the spot, or shortly afterwards, are often valuable
not only in filling gaps in the official records, but in
correcting some of the errors that have worked their
way into those records.

"All this adds up to the conclusion that however
correct Tolstoi's views of the conduct of war may have

been for the early nineteenth century, they are no longer valid. The reason is simple. Technological improvements in communications have made it possible for the historian if not the commander to see pretty well what went on in the heat of battle, since the facts or reported facts upon which the commander based his judgments are on the record. The historian can examine this record at leisure, collate it with other records, and submit it to the usual tests of historical evidence.

"The whole 'truth' may not emerge, but I submit that we arrive at as good an approximation of it as is possible in the writing of any kind of history."[6]

To put this in the words of another of my colleagues: "For the historian the fog of war is no thicker than the fog of politics."[7]

---

[6] "Some Reflections on Method in Military Historiography," Memorandum for the author, 3 March 1953. Files of the Office of the Chief of Military History.

[7] Louis Morton, "The Pacific War and the Historical Program," a memorandum for the author, 4 March 1953. *Ibid.*

II

DORNOT: PUSHING HISTORY
INTO THE FOG OF BATTLE

AN ACTION described in one of our recently published volumes will show what we have been able to do with battle fog.[1]

The author, Charles B. MacDonald, used the types of evidence to which I have referred in the foregoing pages. Having himself commanded a company in the U. S. 2d Infantry Division in Europe, he knew well how battle records are made and what their short-comings are.

The action took place early in September 1944, at the end of the famous race across France of General Patton's Third Army. By September 1, when the Americans had expected to be closing up to the west bank of the Seine to prepare for a long battle, both the First and Third Armies were far beyond it. The Third Army was over the Meuse River and past Verdun, where the Germans had sustained and inflicted over 600,000 casualties when they tried to get past it in 1916. Ahead of Patton were the Moselle, in its deep valley, the rough Sarre River country, the Siegfried line, and the cold rains of the North European au-

[1] "Arnaville," in Charles B. MacDonald and Sidney Mathews, *Three Battles* (Washington, 1952), pp. 1-39, *United States Army in World War II.*

tumn.[2] Audacious, elated, flushed with optimism, and impatient, General Patton on September 6 grandly gave his Army the Rhine from Mainz to Karlsruhe as its objective.[3] At this point the fog originated that enshrouded the battle of Dornot in uncertainties which were brushed aside in the interest of speed.

Patton counted on the complete demoralization of the enemy. Actually the Germans were rapidly assembling ahead of him a combat-worthy force in almost the strength of an army. Furthermore, his route of advance from the Moselle to the Rhine lay through a region which for centuries the French and Germans had fought over and fortified, since through it passed the only practicable lines of communication between central France and central Germany. On the western node of these routes and immediately ahead of him on the Moselle River sat the fortified hedgehog of Metz, ringed with a wide semicircle of forts in front of the city and west of the river. General Patton refused to take seriously the fortifications of Metz, about which he knew only what could be learned from descriptions and plans dating from 1940, and which he believed the Germans could not or would not vigorously defend.

On September 1 General Patton's racing columns had ground to a stop from a drought of gasoline. As soon as gas began to flow again, five days later, General Patton started for the Moselle. He was no longer

2 See map sketch, pp. 48-49.
3 For a full account of this and the subsequent operations of Patton's Army, see Hugh M. Cole, *The Lorraine Campaign* (Washington, 1950) in *United States Army in World War II*.

on terrain where his motorized forces could make wide end runs. He was entering a corridor. But he determined that if Metz did not fall "like a ripe plum," he would by-pass it, to the north and south, leaving the fortress-city to wither on the tree.

To perform this mission he used the XX Corps, commanded by Major General Walton H. Walker, who was later to command the Eighth Army in Korea. General Walker had in his Corps three divisions, including the 7th Armored and the 5th Infantry Division. He chose the 7th Armored Division to spearhead his advance, and before daylight on the sixth of September that division started to roll forward in multiple columns on a broad front. Before nightfall the armor ran up against the wide semicircle of fortified positions in front of Metz, and found that the Germans were determined to defend them stubbornly.

Probing at this ring, the division's Combat Command B bored its way through a chink in the ring to the southwest of Metz. Sneaking past German defenders in the darkness, one of its columns, commanded by Brigadier General John B. Thompson, got down to the west bank of the river at the little village of Dornot. As soon as daylight came on September 7 the Germans began to pound this force with artillery fire and counterattacks. It was able to hold its own, with heavy losses. But, with regard to his mission of getting across the Moselle, all General Thompson could do on the seventh was to send over a little patrol in the three assault boats that were available. This patrol was quickly all but annihilated. Germans on the far shore destroyed two of the boats with machine-gun fire, killed most of the men and drove the survivors back. Nevertheless, hard pressed as he was, General Thompson began to prepare the shattered infantry of his command, the 23d Armored Infantry Battalion, to attempt a crossing the next day (September 8). Since he could use only infantry for the attempt, he ordered his tanks, which had been crowding down the defiles to the river, to clear the area during the night.[4]

Meanwhile, a fresh wave of confusion or, if you please, battle fog, was being generated and projected towards the scene by orders issuing from XX Corps headquarters.

The 5th Infantry Division, commanded by Major General S. LeRoy Irvin, had been following the 7th Armored Division towards Metz, with vague orders from XX Corps headquarters to "pin onto" the tail of the armor. Our historian found out that when General Walker saw that the 7th Armored Division was being held up, he gave an oral order to General Irvin —one of those messages "written on air"—to pass a force from his division through the armored troops and establish a bridgehead across the Moselle opposite Dornot. But General Walker did not rescind his order to the 7th Armored Division to cross the river. Therefore, two of his subordinate commanders, General Irvin and General Thompson, understood themselves to be under orders to do the same thing at the same place. Except by conjecture we have not been able to penetrate this particular fog in corps headquarters. All we know is that that headquarters had received a garbled version of the disastrous attempt of

4 See map sketch, p. 19.

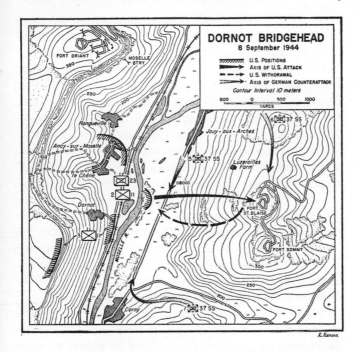

General Thompson's tiny patrol to get across the river and believed that on the seventh he had established a toehold on the east bank. This would explain why General Walker did not rescind his order to the 7th Armored Division. The order he had given General Irvin was to cross and exploit the toehold won by General Thompson's armor. This toehold did not exist.

General Irvin in turn ordered the 11th Infantry Regiment, commanded by Colonel Yuill, to effect the crossing at Dornot for the 5th Division. To carry out

his mission Colonel Yuill sent forward two of his battalions, the 2d and the 3d. The 3d reached the river
south of Dornot at Arnaville and found it unoccu-
pied. The 2d Battalion headed for Dornot. They
found the steep access road clogged with General
Thompson's tanks and night overtook them. Rain began to fall and turned the road into a slippery ribbon.
When they got to Dornot, they found General Thompson trying to prepare his decimated infantry battalion
to get across on the eighth. Each force was completely
surprised to find the other on the scene. Each commander, General Thompson and Colonel Yuill, believed that he was authorized to conduct the crossing
commanding the troops of the other.

Here was fog, indeed, and what happened from this
point on might never have been known but for interviews with those present, since each of the two divisions, in its official report, represents the planning and
execution of the Dornot crossing as its own.

During the night of the seventh both General
Thompson and Colonel Yuill strove to round up support elements, artillery, engineers, medics, assault
boats, from corps reserves and from the reserves of
their two divisions. Colonel Yuill, although made responsible by General Irvin for establishing a bridgehead opposite Dornot, bowed to the fact that General
Thompson was the senior officer in the area, and
quickly recognized that the crossing would therefore
have to be directed by coordination of their efforts.
The records show that at the top no genuine coordination was achieved. But our historians found that the
officers on the ground at Dornot, including General

Thompson, acted on the central fact that emerged from the confusion, namely, that only Colonel Yuill's 2d Battalion had the strength necessary to make an assault crossing. They now bent all their efforts around this fact. General Thompson, after calling in vain for assault boats, himself went into the rear area during the night to round them up.

It soon became evident that the crossing could not be made under cover of darkness as Colonel Yuill had hoped. Actually it was nearly noon on the eighth before enough artillery and assault boats could be brought up to launch the crossing with any hope of success. Meanwhile troops on the ledge by the river at Dornot were not only being harassed by fire from the Germans on their north flank but plastered with well-directed artillery fire which was reducing their strength and hampering their movements. They did not know where this fire was coming from and were not to find out for two days. Actually it was being delivered from three powerful forts on the heights above them to the northwest. These forts were not on the small-scale maps which had been issued to the regimental officers, and higher headquarters had issued no information about them. Not until the evening of the ninth did a patrol discover the existence of the mightiest of them, Fort Driant, and then learned only that it was a fort. Fort Driant was in fact so powerful and well defended that it was not silenced until two months later.

Shortly after noon on the eighth, just as the crossing finally got under way under heavy fire, General Thompson was ordered to report to 7th Armored Di-

vision headquarters. "Here he was relieved of command and subsequently reduced in rank. One of the
reasons given for his relief was that Combat Command
B had established a bridgehead across the Moselle on
7 September and then had withdrawn it contrary to
the orders of the XX Corps Commander."[5] This, as
we have seen, was not a fact. Confusion on high levels
had now claimed the only officer above the rank of
lieutenant-colonel who had even seen the crossing site
at Dornot. (General Thompson was later exonerated
and restored to the rank of brigadier general.)

In the crossing that began at noon on the eighth
the 2d Battalion of the 11th Infantry, with some men
of the 23d Armored Infantry Battalion among them,
got across the river, under heavy rifle, machine-gun,
mortar, and artillery fire. Once across, they sought
refuge from this fire in a horseshoe-shaped patch of
woods opposite the crossing site and reorganized for
action.

Above them, mounted on the crest of a steep slope,
were Fort Blaise and Fort Sommy. The Americans
knew that these forts were there and that they must
be taken, but knew nothing more about them. In the
late afternoon two companies, "F" and "G," were sent
up the long slope to take Fort Blaise. It was strangely
silent. "Company F slowly and methodically cut its
way through five separate double-apron barbed wire
obstacles, only to come up against an iron portcullis
studded with curved iron hooks." Beyond this was a
deep moat. Above the moat loomed "a huge domed

5 MacDonald, "Arnaville," p. 21.

structure of three large casemates constructed of concrete and covered by grassy earth."[6]

On September 8 this monster was manned only by a weak security detachment which withdrew as the Americans approached. But the 2d Batallion did not know this, and the Captain of Company F, pulling his men back 400 yards, called for artillery fire to crack the fort.

It came promptly, but the 2d Battalion could no longer concern itself with the forts on the crest. For the Germans, alerted by the arrival of the Americans at Dornot, had quickly brought up a powerful panzer battalion to reinforce the weak formations in the area, which had been thrown into confusion by the crossing. Two columns of enemy tanks and infantry were now bearing down, one from the north, the other from the south, on the horseshoe woods, where the Americans were hastily digging in and organizing a perimeter defense. The converging columns threatened to cut off the two companies up the slope. Only when darkness closed in were the survivors of the two companies able to scramble into the perimeter.

The hail of shells from Fort Driant had defeated the efforts of the Engineers to construct a bridge across the river. No tanks could be put into the bridgehead. So accurate and deadly was the shelling that boats could cross only at night.

The little horseshoe woods opposite Dornot now became the scene of a defense as heroic as can be found in the annals of American arms. The Germans

6 MacDonald, "Arnaville," pp. 23-24.

hit it again and again with tanks and infantry. In the darkness, "the defenders could hear shouted orders followed by almost fanatical charges with the enemy bunched and yelling. The American automatic rifles had a field day," and with the help of artillery from the west shore turned back every attack. "The woods were filled with cries for medics. Realizing that such calls would disclose positions, Sergeant Hembree, Company E, sent around an order that no one was to cry out. The exhibition of self-discipline that followed was one of the heartening feats of courage during the hectic days in the bridgehead."

"During the first night counterattacks, two men of Company K, Pfc. George T. Dickey and Pfc. Frank Lalopa, who had volunteered to man an outpost beyond the main line of resistance, stuck to their post despite a warning order to withdraw. Armed only with M-1 rifles, the two men held off the enemy until finally they were surrounded and killed. The next morning when other men of Company K crawled out to the position, they found the bodies of twenty-two Germans, some within three yards of the bodies of Dickey and Lalopa."[7]

During the next two days and nights the enemy hurled attack after attack against the little bridgehead —an estimated thirty-six in all. The force of many of these was broken by our artillery, now massed on the heights above the west bank and accurately directed by forward observers, through a system of radio communications that never failed. It was an infantry-

[7] MacDonald, "Arnaville," pp. 26-27.

artillery team that stopped the enemy. This detracts nothing from the glory of the men inside the perimeter of the horseshoe woods. The heroism with which they stuck to their unenviable task was clearly illustrated by an event on the third day of the fight. Although it was obvious to anyone who knew the local situation that the little perimeter defense could not hold out much longer, the defenders on the morning of September 10 called on the Germans to surrender. They warned them that if they did not capitulate the Americans would bring down on them such a concentration of fire as they had never seen. This splendid bit of bravado we would, by the way, not have known about but for the German records. Our own do not mention it.

As the days passed, while German shellfire continued to pummel the crossing site, the hope of getting reinforcements into the bridgehead faded and then went out. Ammunition, food, and water could be got in and the wounded evacuated only in little rubber assault boats and only at night. General Irvin told the men to hold out as best they could while he threw another force across the river opposite the village of Arnaville. Once that position was secure, the little force opposite Dornot might be pulled out. On September 10 word came at last to withdraw the men from the horseshoe woods. Plans went forward for slipping them back to the west bank after dark.

In the meantime, unaware of the impending withdrawal, the Germans had issued an order for an all-out assault against the little bridgehead that same night. The German signal for shifting their artillery forward to cover this assault was to be a green flare. By coincidence, we had also decided on a green flare as the signal that the withdrawal of our men had been completed. When our flare went up, American artillery was to plaster the horseshoe woods in the hope of catching enemy forces that probably would move into the woods as soon as ours pulled out.

The last boatloads and swimmers were reaching the west bank. Then, as a lieutenant charged with the firing of the American flare checked the woods to make sure everybody had got out, the Germans shot their green signal flare. The lieutenant and his communications sergeant, knowing that no matter who had fired the green flare the American artillery would quickly respond, scrambled into their little rubber boat and paddled furiously back toward the west bank. They made it as the first rounds from both German and American artillery pounded the horseshoe woods and the river.

Long after the fighting was over, one of our historical officers collected the testimony of the last American witness of what happened on the far shore on that grim night. It reveals a strange chance of battle. It also throws a gleam of light on what our artillery, called down by the green flare of the Germans, did to the enemy troops whom that flare inadvertently summoned to their death in the area.

"Despite precautions to see that no men were left in the bridgehead, at least one man, Pvt. Joseph I. Lewakowski, Company G, had either fallen asleep or lost consciousness in his foxhole about fifty yards from the river. He awoke the next morning just as day was breaking. Climbing from his covered foxhole to find himself alone, he 'walked across dead Germans from his foxhole to the river bank.' (These German dead may have been casualties from American artillery fire called down by the German signal flare.)" Pvt. Lewakowski pulled himself across the river to Dornot by a rope that had been left in position on just such a chance that some American might still be on the far shore. By now the Americans had pulled out of Dornot. But Pvt. Lewakowski got something to eat, then found a bed and went back to sleep, and on the following night "made his way to the rear and rejoined his company."[8]

In the days of my boyhood, when societies that met to discuss Robert Browning's obscure poetry were numerous, someone said of them: "Browning societies are like foghorns. They call attention to fog but do nothing to dispel it." Certainly our narratives call attention to the fog of battle. But it can be said, further, that they show that some of it is preventable. It can be seen from the story just related that they have been able to disclose in considerable detail what went on under its cover.

---

[8] MacDonald, "Arnaville," pp. 37-38. The final incident in Pvt. Lewakowski's highly personal withdrawal from the scene of action was related to Mr. MacDonald in a letter from an officer of the company after he had read MacDonald's original account.

III

COALITION STRATEGY:
THE ARMY'S OUTLOOK

STRATEGY is a subject in the history of war that fasci-
nates many people who think of it as being concerned
with very high and mysterious considerations. Actually
the secrets of Allied strategy in World War II have
been disclosed in so many books that there is already
less mystery about it than about many other aspects of
the war. Furthermore, this book is focused on the
Army, and our strategy was not made by the Army.
But the high command of our Army had much to do
with shaping strategy, and the historians of *United
States Army in World War II* have had to deal with it,
from a variety of angles. Their findings on the subject
permit me to offer some reflections on the way we
made war in 1942-1945 which seem to me to be of considerable importance to thoughtful Americans.

Strategy is a three-plied word. It connotes concepts
—strategic concepts. It connotes also the plans of a
power or coalition of powers for imposing its will on
the enemy. Finally, it connotes the use of means which
proved successful or unsuccessful in accomplishing this
purpose.

Let me say at once that the theme that I shall under-
take to illustrate in what follows is that both the
strategic plans and the strategic measures of the Allies

in World War II were hammered out on the anvil of necessity. What I believe to have been the principal contribution of the United States Army to the result will become clear, I hope, as I go.

As early as January 1941 representatives of the military staffs of the United States and Great Britain, conferring secretly in Washington, made two strategic decisions that were of momentous importance. One was that if the United States was forced to enter the war the common objective of this country and Great Britain would be the defeat of the nations arrayed against them, even if these, as seemed not unlikely, should include Japan. The other decision was that if Japan entered the war, the Allies would defeat the European Axis first, remaining on the defensive in the Pacific until they had done this. They would treat Germany as their "Number 1" enemy; only after defeating Germany would they go all out against Japan. Both of these decisions, then purely military, were subsequently adopted as the national policy of the United States.[1]

These two decisions, reiterated, were the foundation stones of the strategic planning of the Allies. They contained the principles by which the political and military leaders of the United States and Great Britain

[1] Well-informed accounts of these military conversations, eventuating in the agreement known as ABC-1, can be found in Maurice Matloff and Edwin M. Snell, *Strategic Planning for Coalition Warfare, 1941-1942* (Washington, 1953), Chapter III, pp. 32-42; and Mark S. Watson, *Chief of Staff: Pre-War Plans and Preparations* (Washington, 1950), Chap. XII, both in *United States Army in World War II*.

measured and endeavored to shape their plans in World War II.

The first of these two decisions was nothing if not an expression of bold military thinking, given the circumstances under which it was first made, in January 1941. Great Britain was then standing alone. Its ground forces had been stripped of their equipment, left behind on the beaches at Dunkerque. Its homeland was being unmercifully bombed and was believed to be in danger of invasion by the Germans. The Soviet Union was bound to Hitler by a pact of neutrality. The military power of the United States was pitifully feeble, and its Government was bound over to keep the peace by a public overwhelmingly reluctant to become involved in war.

The point that stands out boldly is that adherence to the principle then declared, and later adopted by the nation, committed the United States to an unlimited war both in the Atlantic and the Pacific. Japan never planned to wage an unlimited war; when Hitler and Mussolini set forth on their career of international crime, they did so with the declared object of acquiring *Lebensraum*—more space in which to flourish— and Hitler continued to believe that he could acquire this short of crushing his opponents. The object which the United States, Great Britain, and the Soviet Union avowed from the outset and consistently pursued was not the occupation of territory but war to the death against their enemies.

These basic decisions, although momentous in effect, contained only vague and general indications of the way in which they could be carried out. They embodied only strategic concepts. To be carried out they had to be translated into strategic plans.

World War II was a period during which the manufacture of strategic plans became a major industry of our military establishment.[2] The study of these innumerable plans has fascinated our historians, partly perhaps because of the secrecy with which they were surrounded during the war, and the excitement of being allowed to explore them. The history of this peculiar war industry falls into two different periods. One extends to the summer of 1943, more precisely to the Allied Conference at Quebec in August 1943; the second to the end of the war.

When the first period began, Great Britain stood alone. In June 1941 Russia joined her, in December 1941 the United States. The second period began when Great Britain and the United States, in the summer of 1943, had mastered the submarine, thrown their enemies on the defensive both in Western Europe and the Pacific, and acquired the means by which they might hope to defeat them. Their strategic planning to that end became from that point on of a different order of importance.

In the first period most of their effective planning consisted of the almost desperate business of matching means to ends to meet situations of apparently extreme danger. The Western Allies had to do two things at once, and given the situation in December 1941, both

[2] For the Army's mechanism used by General Marshall to manufacture and coordinate strategic plans, see Ray S. Cline, *Washington Command Post: the Operations Division,* Washington, 1951, *United States Army in World War II.*

were tasks so tremendous and so hard to perform
simultaneously that our enemies believed them to be
beyond the powers of the United States and Great
Britain to achieve, and all the more difficult because
they had to be achieved by a coalition. With one hand
the Allies had to draw a ring (actually two rings)
around the outward thrust of their two powerful enemies and hold these rings; with the other they had to
build up their power to take the offensive themselves
on two fronts separated by half the globe. In early
1942 some of the coolest military heads in the United
States believed that the United Nations were on "the
verge of ultimate defeat."[3]

During this period the Western Allies did what they
could, rather than what they wanted to do. As soon as
Japan pitched us into the war, the British and American governments, now openly allied, reiterated their
determination to wage unlimited war and to defeat
Germany first.[4] They pooled all their munitions and
their means of producing and transporting them, and
created an unprecedented common authority, the
Combined Chiefs of Staff, which was to hammer out
their strategy, direct their military efforts, and allocate
the resources with which they were to carry them out.
The immediate task of the Allies was not strategy in
any but a hand-to-mouth sense; it was to concert a

[3] From a paper of the Joint U. S. Strategic Committee, JPS 2/5,
6 Mar. 42, cited in Richard M. Leighton and Robert Coakley,
Logistics of Global Warfare, 1940-1943 (a forthcoming volume in
United States Army in World War II), Chap. XIV.

[4] At the so-called ARCADIA Conference, described in Matloff and
Snell, *Strategic Planning*, Chapter V.

series of measures that seemed necessary to avert defeat.[5]

For the United States the first and most urgent task as the nation awoke, shamed and outraged by the smoking wreckage of Pearl Harbor, was to secure Hawaii, the Panama Canal, and the West Coast. For the next six months we felt it necessary to throw our meager quota of ready forces into the task of containing the still expanding thrust of the Japanese into Southeast Asia. This meant turning Australia into a great base of operations and keeping open to it a line of communications over 6,000 miles long. Meanwhile all we could do in the submarine-infested Atlantic was to help the British to keep our lines of communication with England and Russia open, and give those two hard-pressed nations everything we could spare without yielding the Pacific to Japan and without bringing to a stop the formation and training of the formidable ground, air, and naval forces that we were constructing in the United States.

Almost a year before the end of this first period, the Allies began to achieve successes that still seem astonishing. In the Pacific as early as May 1942 the remnant of the United States Fleet, from the flight decks of its carriers, checked the Japanese in the Battle of the Coral Sea. A month later the Navy and shore-based air inflicted a decisive defeat on the main body of the Japanese Navy in the Battle of Midway. Immediately, our combined forces in the Pacific went over to the

[5] The frantic splicing and patching to make ends meet in 1942 is described fully in Leighton and Coakley, *Logistics of Global Warfare, 1941-1943*, Chaps. VI-VII, XIV-XXI.

offensive. General MacArthur, launching an attack from Port Moresby, drove the Japanese back on Buna, and in January 1943 forced them to abandon the eastern tip of New Guinea. Simultaneously the Navy landed the 1st Marine Division on Guadalcanal and seized its airfield, and by June 1943 a combined Army-Navy force had begun to drive the enemy back towards Rabaul, his great forward base in the South Pacific. Meanwhile in the Atlantic a great Anglo-American amphibious force had occupied North Africa. In May 1943, linked with the victorious British Eighth Army, it captured Tunis and rounded up some 250,000 Axis prisoners. In July another amphibious expedition overran Sicily in thirty-eight days; Mussolini was overthrown, and on September 8 the Royal Italian Government announced its surrender.

But in these successes the American Army felt that the Allies, while effectively using their forces to do what they could, were not doing what, in the view of the American Joint Chiefs of Staff, the Allies ought to be doing. The outlook of the Army on strategy became clearly defined in the inter-Allied discussions in which its representatives tried, in vain, to get the British to accept their view.

A study of the Army's strategic planning during this period shows that its leaders were urgently intent on the adoption of two principles as necessary if the Allies were to win:

(*1*) They must, at the earliest practicable moment, launch power-drives at the heart of their enemies' positions.

(2) They must decide long in advance what these

power-drives would be, at what objectives they were to be aimed, where they were to be mounted, and at what date they were to be launched. In short, a definite strategic plan must be agreed on and put into effect at once. In this view the Navy was at one with the War Department, in spirit and in principle.

Before going further it is important to add that from December 7, 1941, the strategic thinking of the Army and Navy was founded on a belief that by mid-1943 the United States would be ready to furnish enough men and materiel to enable the Allies to contain the Japanese in the Pacific and launch the power-drive in Europe which the Army regarded as necessary to defeat the Axis.

Its confidence that this would be possible was based on a farsighted survey of resources that had been undertaken in the fall of 1941. This was the so-called Victory Program, presented to Mr. Roosevelt in September of that year.[6]

It was Mr. Roosevelt, not General Marshall, who called for this Program. It was a far-reaching and gigantic attempt to calculate the forces and the production that would be necessary to defeat all the possible enemies of Great Britain and the United States if these two powers became jointly engaged in the war. The Army's contribution to the Victory Program was an attempt to nail this vastly complex calculation to a strategy regarded by it as necessary to defeat these ene-

[6] This is discussed in Watson, *Chief of Staff*, Chap. VI; more fully in Leighton and Coakley, *Logistics*, Chap. V. See also William L. Langer and S. Everett Gleason, *The Undeclared War* (Washington, 1953) pp. 735-42.

mies, including Japan. For the purpose of the present
discussion, the most important features of this strategic blueprint were two. It assumed that massive land
offensives would be required, first against the Axis,
eventually against Japan. It further assumed that the
Soviet Union would be defeated by the Nazis and that
the Atlantic Allies would have to cope with all the
remaining forces of the Axis.

For the future the most consequential feature of the
Victory Program was that, almost at once, the American productive economy and plans for the completion
of an American military force were geared to this
vastly ambitious program, and after Pearl Harbor,
though the machine did not run smoothly at first, it
was thrown into high gear. The eventual consequences
were immense. One was that when the Soviet armies,
far from accepting defeat, rebounded from Stalingrad
and went over to the offensive in 1943, the Allies soon
had both the forces and supplies necessary to give
effect to the American concept of power-drives against
the citadels of both of their enemies.

American industry would, and did, supply the munitions and equipment. That by 1943 we had the troops
under arms and the air force necessary to support our
concepts of strategy is to be attributed to the size and
nature of the forces that the War Department began to
mobilize in the United States as early as the summer
of 1940. Throughout that year and 1941 the strategic
mission of the Army was the defense of the Western
Hemisphere. Hemispheric (rather than continental)
defense Mr. Roosevelt had declared to be the policy
of the United States on the ground that air power had

brought the bulge of Brazil within the striking range of a hostile European power basing itself on the Atlantic coast of North Africa. The War Department, although defense thus conceived was its mission, proceeded from the first to build up and train land and air forces designed to be powerful enough to carry out the American concept of offensive strategy, in alliance with Great Britain, if the United States should be drawn into the war. It was possible to do this in spite of our prevailing isolation, since an Army of 1,400,000, with a possible augmentation bringing it up to 2,800,000 by the end of 1942, was regarded as necessary to defend the Western Hemisphere should Great Britain go under and the United States be left standing alone.[7]

But the Army that was being constructed contained powerful offensive forces, was largely motorized, and included two elements of great striking power: a large armored force and a mighty air force. Mr. Roosevelt's bold decision greatly to enlarge the Army's air component, rather than follow General Marshall's plan for a powerful but balanced force, increased the capacity of the Army, as planned, to implement an offensive strategy. A powerful strategic bombing force was the dearest object of General Arnold's young and ambitious Army Air Forces, created in June 1941. A strategic bombing force, which is nothing if not an offensive force, would both lengthen and strengthen the

[7] These decisions and measures are set forth under the light of fresh documentation in Stetson Conn and Byron Fairchild, *The Framework of Hemisphere Defense,* a forthcoming volume in *United States Army in World War II.*

arm by which a blow could be dealt at the heart of the enemy.

During 1941 the Army's effort to build up forces capable of decisive offensive action was gravely compromised and apparently endangered by the "Arsenal of Democracy" policy, at last freely implemented in March 1941 by the Lend-Lease Act. This policy gave the nations fighting Hitler and Mussolini first claim on all supplies and military equipment being produced in the United States except such as our military authorities declared indispensable to the defense of the Western Hemisphere. The War Department now had not only to face the competition of these powers for American productive facilities, but saw the artillery, the tanks, the trucks, the airplanes produced to fill their own orders being creamed off to arm and equip the British and later the Russians (and Chinese) as well. The policy made sense. It seemed just possible, after Hitler involved himself with Russia in 1941, that Lend-Lease might permit the United States to avoid getting into the war. In any case, it would lengthen the time given us to prepare for the worst, meanwhile strengthening our base for the production of war goods. But it threatened to bring to a stop the effort of the War Department to train and equip an effective force of our own. The effect was so serious that in the spring of 1941 the effort to ready a single small task force, with the mission of occupying positions in the Azores, had strained to the limit the resources that the armed forces could at that moment command. Then in September General Marshall, to his dismay, was faced by the President with a proposal to cut the Army's authorized strength, in order to give more aid to Britain and Russia.[8] The President withdrew it, and Pearl Harbor resolved the issue, leaving no doubt that eventually we were to have a powerful force of our own and also aid the anti-Axis powers. But in the fall of 1941 the goal of having forces capable of supporting an offensive strategy seemed to have receded into a vague and distant future.

Enough men and enough resources were the eventual consequences of the basic decisions made in 1941. But the immediate effect of the storm that broke on December 7, 1941, was swiftly to carry the Americans farther still from their goal of concentration and powerful blows. For the next six months everything the Army and Navy had that was ready had to go into the Pacific to stop Japan. The winter and spring of 1942 was a period of terrific stress and anxiety.

Yet in the midst of this disheartening situation the War Department made a strategic proposal, the audacity of which fully disclosed the basic drives in American military thought.

Brigadier General Dwight D. Eisenhower had been summoned to Washington by General Marshall in December 1941 to direct the task of securing the line to Australia and turning that subcontinent into a base of operations against the Japanese. The group of able young officers in the War Department, of whom Eisen-

---

[8] But not immediately, since aid to our Allies was stepped up and laid fresh claims on the production of munitions needed to ready our own forces. Leighton and Coakley, *Logistics*, Chaps. VIII and X. On the President's proposal, Conn and Fairchild, *Western Hemisphere*, Chap. VI, corrects Watson's account, *Chief of Staff*, pp. 363-66.

hower was soon made Chief—the Operations Division of the General Staff—watched with increasing dismay the piecemeal commitment and dissipation of our forces. They saw that unless checked it would inevitably deprive the United States of the power to throw a decisive weight into the defeat of the Axis, or to exercise a decisive influence in favor of the strategy without which they believed it could not be accomplished.[9]

In March General Marshall, acting on their advice, decided that the only hope of saving the principle of concentration of force was to get the British committed to a definite and dated plan for hitting the Nazis and hitting them hard, and to begin at once to commit to it the forces and supplies necessary to carry it out. These were to be prepared and concentrated in England on the basis of a priority overriding every other demand except such as had to be met to keep the Axis or the Japanese from breaking through the rings then being drawn around them.

This daring proposal had the strong support of Secretary Stimson, of General Arnold, and of the Navy, now led by Admiral King. In April the President sent General Marshall and Harry Hopkins to London to get the British to accept it.[10]

[9] Matloff and Snell, *Strategic Planning*, pp. 87 ff. and Chap. VII. The outlook of the Army planners from the outset is sharply reflected in the entry General Eisenhower made in his notebook on January 22, 1942: "The struggle to secure adoption by all concerned of a common concept of strategical objectives is wearing me down. . . . We've got to go to Europe and fight. . . . We've got to begin slugging with air at West Europe; to be followed by a land attack as soon as possible."

[10] The reader interested in an account of this mission and in an elaboration of the points that follow in the text should con-

The nub of the American plan was to launch a powerful attack against Germany through the Channel Coast of France in April 1943. As their contribution the Americans promised that by that date they would put in England thirty divisions, 3,250 combat aircraft, and the supplies necessary to support them, and that beginning at once they would build up there a great force of bombers to join the RAF in preparing the way by a massive assault on Germany from the air. The American plan included the even bolder proposal that the Allies should immediately prepare to launch a cross-Channel attack in September 1942 (SLEDGEHAMMER) if either the Russians or the Germans by that time showed signs of caving in. The object in the first case would be, if possible, to save the Russians. If, on the other hand, the Nazis suddenly and unexpectedly weakened, the object would be to make sure that an Allied force was in on the kill.

Mr. Churchill and the British Chiefs of Staff immediately accepted the plan in principle. SLEDGEHAMMER, the bold secondary feature of the American plan, shocked them, and although at first they rolled with the punch and accepted it as part of the package, they soon decided that SLEDGEHAMMER would be suicidal. In retrospect SLEDGEHAMMER seems important for two

---

sult, for American views: Matloff and Snell, *Strategic Planning*, Chaps. VIII, XII, and XIII (the most thorough study to date); Harrison, *Cross-Channel Attack*, Chap. I; Robert E. Sherwood, *Roosevelt and Hopkins* (New York, 1948), Chaps. XXIII and XXV; Henry L. Stimson and McGeorge Bundy, *On Active Service* (New York, 1947), Chap. XVII; for the British side, Winston Churchill, *The Hinge of Fate* (Boston, 1940), Book I, Chap. 18, and Book II, Chap. 2.

reasons. It expressed the offensive determination of the Americans, and it convinced the British that American military thought was dangerously optimistic and reckless.

The best argument for an attack through France in 1943 was that it would permit the strongest concentration, possibly a decisive concentration, of Allied forces on the shortest line of approach to the heart of Germany. Utilizing England as the base of concentration, and as a vast airplane carrier, it would reinforce the defense of England during the build-up, while attack from any other base would require the diversion of forces from the defense of England. Since England was on the comparatively short North Atlantic line of communication from the American "arsenal," utilization of England as a base would permit the most economical use of the scarcest resource of all, troop and cargo shipping, with which to deliver the maximum contribution of American men and machines and material.

The decision to go ahead with the plan brought relief to the War Department if only because it gave General Marshall and his staff a means of heading off the constant dissipation of men and means that had become a nightmare to them. They were able now to commit these in accordance with a scheduled build-up in England (called BOLERO). BOLERO was given top priority and reached back into every training camp and war plant in the United States. General Eisenhower, now Chief of the Operations Division, General Marshall's global "command post," wrote in his notebook on April 20, 1942, when Marshall got back from London: ". . . at long last, and after months of struggle, . . . we are all committed to one concept of fighting! If we can agree on major purposes and objectives, our efforts will begin to fall in line and we won't just be thrashing around in the dark."[11]

The relief and happiness in the War Department did not last long. In July the British declared that SLEDGEHAMMER was impracticable and refused to support it. Thereupon President Roosevelt and Mr. Churchill decided to use all their available forces, including those being accumulated in England for BOLERO, to go into the Mediterranean and occupy French North Africa. The President's decision, which Mr. Churchill had sought with all his might and main, was one of the few strategic decisions Mr. Roosevelt made during the war in which he overruled his military chiefs. His reason was that he wanted American ground forces to become heavily engaged with the enemy in 1942, and North Africa was the only place that offered a prospect of doing this with good hope of success in damaging the Axis. The result was TORCH, which began on November 8, 1942. It culminated in a resounding Anglo-American victory in Tunis. But this was not achieved until May 1943.

The decision for TORCH precipitated a debate on strategy between the Americans and the British, and to a lesser degree within the counsels of each Ally. This lasted until the decision to attack Hitler through France was made final and firm by the appointment of

[11] Quoted in Matloff and Snell, *Strategic Planning,* p. 190. The evolution of the Operations Division as an instrument of global command is described in Cline, *Washington Command Post.*

a supreme commander, General Eisenhower, in December 1943.

Space does not permit me to follow this grand debate, round by round.[12] The simplest way to state the issue in controversy is to oppose two expressions. One, Mr. Churchill's, is "closing the ring"; the other, representing the American view, is "concentration on a penetrating thrust." It was not a question of passing to the offensive: the British were as intent on that as we were. But the British idea was to use the forces of the Allies as they accumulated in jabs all around "the ring," with forces capable of hitting hard, but so used as to be able to disengage and hit again somewhere else. Meanwhile, the Allies would back the Soviets to the limit with supplies and equipment; achieve complete domination of the seas; tighten the blockade of the Axis; bomb its vitals and the morale of its people from the air; give aid to guerrillas and other elements of internal resistance in all occupied areas, and continually encourage these with propaganda. Having thus worn the enemy down until he was weak, they would finally move in for the kill with an offensive directed at some vital point in his territory. The Americans wanted to use all these means but never at the expense of building up and concentrating for a power-drive at the earliest possible date with forces capable of striking

12 For what follows, Churchill's *Closing The Ring* (New York, 1953) should be added to the books cited in Note 10; also Gordon Harrison, "Operation OVERLORD," transcript of an address given at the Army War College, November 19, 1951 (OCMH Files), a brilliant presentation of the "power-drive" vs. "mop-up" conception as a key to the Anglo-American debate over strategy in this period.

directly and decisively at the heart of the enemy's power. "The Americans believed and consistently maintained that Germany's defeat 'could only be effected by direct military action' and that that action must be directed against the main body of the German army in the West."[13]

As I have said, the decision to go into North Africa made the American Chiefs of Staff unhappy, threw their plan of action into disarray,[14] and reopened the prospect of piecemeal applications of force. With the large forces committed in the Mediterranean by TORCH in the spring of 1943, it was hard for the Americans to resist the argument for at least taking Sicily. The Allies, therefore, decided to take Sicily, and they overran it quickly in July. The objective of knocking Italy out of the war had long been agreed on, and Mr. Churchill now won his contention that to do so the Allies must invade that country. This they did in September. The Italian Government surrendered but the Germans moved in and met us on the beaches at Salerno. Mr. Churchill insisted, with success, that the Allies must now do no less than capture Rome, and they became involved in the long, murderous grind of the Italian campaign.

Mr. Roosevelt was in favor of all of these decisions. Mr. Churchill, who, as General Eisenhower has remarked, always saw "great and decisive possibilities in the Mediterranean," rejoiced.[15] The American Chiefs

[13] Harrison, *Cross-Channel Attack,* p. 42.

[14] Matloff and Snell, *Strategic Planning,* Chap. XIV; Leighton and Coakley, *Logistics,* XVI, XVII and XXV.

[15] Dwight D. Eisenhower, *Crusade in Europe* (New York, 1948), p. 194.

of Staff objected at every step. Their position was that
the Mediterranean contained no strategic objectives of
decisive importance, and that the Allied forces were
being pinned down in an indecisive theater by the
weight of their great supply establishments. In the
light of the record to date our historians have con-
cluded that what disturbed the Americans most profoundly was their conviction, now thoroughly established, that the British "attached little importance to
long-range commitments," and were willing to persist
in depending on opportunity.

The disturbance and suspicion of the Americans
were not dissipated when, at the Quebec conference in
August 1943, the British Chiefs and Mr. Churchill
committed themselves to a cross-Channel invasion, to
be launched not later than June 1, 1944. They remem-
bered that the British had committed themselves to
such an invasion before and had retracted. And there
was an "if" attached to British support: they would go
along if the Germans in the spring of 1944 had no
more than twelve mobile divisions in reserve in France
and only if these were so distributed that by D plus 2
not more than five of them could be brought up to
Caen. The concept of opportunism was again raising
its head. It was evident that the British still had no
desire for a power-drive against the Nazis. They
wanted a mop-up.

If to the Americans the British seemed evasive, over-
cautious, wedded to opportunism and unwilling to act
on basic principles, the Americans seemed to the
British to be "militarily unsophisticated," overconfident, and, above all, rigid in their thinking. Mr.

Churchill, in the latest volume of his memoirs, speaks of our "rigid adherence to plans," and our "stern and strict priorities for OVERLORD" (the cross-Channel attack decided on for June 1944). These "were carried in the secondary ranks," he remarks politely but crossly, "to the point of pedantry." In the fall of 1943 Mr. Churchill was fretting and fuming for reinforcement of the campaign in Italy, even at the cost of delaying OVERLORD. General Marshall would not budge. "Here," says Mr. Churchill, "the American clearcut, logical, large-scale, mass-production style of thought was formidable."[16]

We can understand the Anglo-American debate over strategy only if we remember the different traditions and, above all, the different economic systems which the two partners brought to their military collaboration. The British system, unlike ours, had two great complementary centers of gravity. One was the United Kingdom with its industries; the other was in the Far Eastern Dominions and India. The nexus between the two was the Mediterranean. When we entered the war, both centers were mortally threatened, and the Axis powers had cut the connection. The connection was vital. As late as 1940, when the British had resorted to every economy, the home islands were still drawing almost half of their imports, not from nearby sources in the North Atlantic region, but from the Middle and Far East. It is not surprising that Mr. Churchill strove to postpone every other effort until the British had

---

[16] Churchill, *Closing the Ring*, pp. 154, 426. The phrase "militarily unsophisticated" is Chester Wilmot's in *The Struggle for Europe* (New York, 1952), p. 128.

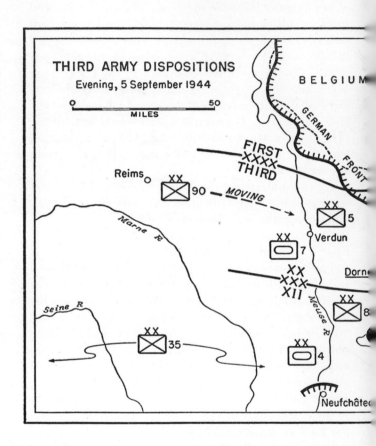

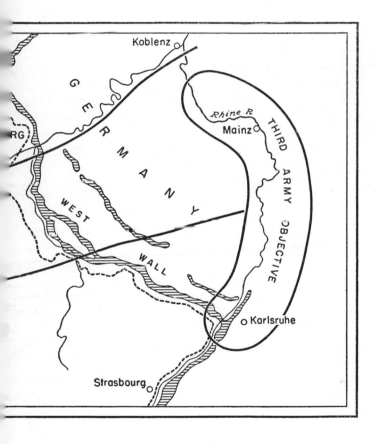

completely recovered their domination of the Mediterranean.[17]

Given their position, it was equally natural that the
British should conceive of strategy primarily in terms
of sea-power, blockade, strangulation, and "closing
the ring," and think of armies, in which they had always been relatively weak, as a force of maneuver, to
be applied sparingly, here and there, and not committed en masse in any one place until, as in the Pen-
insular War in 1813, the opportunity for a decisive
intervention had matured. This was the system they
had used with success since the sixteenth century. They
were using it in World War II when, in spite of their
distaste for Communist Russia, they strained every
nerve to equip and supply the fighting forces of the
USSR from the moment these were committed to fighting Hitler. When they had departed from this system
in World War I and had committed large land forces
in France, the flower of a whole generation of English-
men had been virtually annihilated. The British were
haunted by such slaughters as Passchendaele. This was
one reason why Mr. Churchill was cold to the idea of
a massive cross-Channel attack. "How often have I
heard him say," General Eisenhower reports, " 'We
must take care that the tides do not run red with the
blood of British and American youths, or the beaches
be choked with their bodies.' " He himself has written:
"The fearful price we had had to pay in human blood
and life for the great offensives of the First World War
was graven in my mind."[18]

[17] Leighton and Coakley, *Logistics*, Chap. II.
[18] Eisenhower, *Crusade*, p. 194; Churchill, *Closing the Ring*,
p. 582.

The way in which the Americans insisted on making war, and reacted in debate, likewise can be understood only with reference to their tradition and background. Granting that they were inexperienced in war, and seemed to the British youthfully reckless and overconfident, their faith in our industrial potential proved to be well founded, and their concepts of war-making were based on their knowledge of the nature of that potential and of its relation to mechanized warfare.

The gear of a mechanized army and air force adds up to an enormous load of equipment, and this had to be shipped and established on bases far from the continental United States. For nearly two years after we entered the war, the movement of this load overseas was on a short and precarious tether of shipping. What wonder then that the Americans insisted from the first on a cross-Channel attack through France, since England provided a ready-made base from which to attack and the haul to England was comparatively short? Again, the Americans were keenly aware that under a system of mass production such as ours, a lead time (of from a year to eighteen months) was necessary for the production of the complicated military hardware that modern warfare requires. To this lead time must be added that needed for the amassing and organization of this complex gear in the right quantities and proportion on the base of attack. The Americans soon became highly sensitive, furthermore, to the fact that this vast apparatus, once moved, cannot be readily shifted. And they quickly learned that when a force is once moved overseas, its equipment must be moved with it and supplies to support it must then be kept flowing to it, laying a continuous claim on production in the United States. In the lean and anxious months after Pearl Harbor, when the War Department had to ship out to the Pacific everything it had to plug gaps in the vast ring we were trying to throw around the racing Japanese, it learned, if its officers had not realized it before, that our forces could be fixed by piecemeal, opportunistic commitment, both of troops and supplies, in a pattern that would postpone indefinitely the concentration of these for powerful and decisive blows at the enemy across the Atlantic. The Americans were not doctrinaire when they insisted on firm agreements as to where the decisive attacks were to be made.

When Mr. Churchill, therefore, characterizes General Marshall's undeviating adherence to the execution of the cross-Channel attack in the spring of 1944 as typical of American "mass-production thinking," this amounts to accusing the Americans of having a mass-production economy.[19] That economy imposed a rigidity on our strategic concepts that irked the British, but once American production went into high gear it poured forth results that amazed them. When the British read *The Cross Channel Attack,* by Gordon Harrison, General Sir Frederick Morgan, who drafted the OVERLORD plan, wrote the author that he was shocked to learn with what anxiety and distrust the American military leaders had regarded the supposed intentions of their British opposites. But admitting that the British had likewise at first distrusted the proposals of the American Chiefs of Staff, he ob-

19 Harrison, "Operation OVERLORD."

served that it was because when the Americans made their bold proposals for body blows at the enemy, the British, remembering World War I, had no idea that we could produce the divisions, air forces, and equipment necessary to carry them out. They tended, not unnaturally, to regard us as boastful, inexperienced and reckless children. When the men and materiel began to appear overseas according to promise, the picture changed. Given the nature and organization of the American industrial economy, and given the extent to which the outcome of the whole Allied effort depended on the mass production of complex and specialized implements of war, it can be argued that the American military chiefs, far from being rigid theorists, were guided by practical sense in insisting on steadfast adherence to large and definite objectives, as well as in their belief that such objectives could be won.

Finally, the American strategic outlook cannot be understood without remembering the Pacific. The war in that area was the one in which the American public was really interested. Furthermore, by agreement with the British, that war was our responsibility. As previously remarked, the offensive spirit and capabilities of the American Army and Navy asserted themselves in the Pacific with surprising speed. General MacArthur was nothing if not offensively-minded. He never bowed to the Allied decision that Germany was the "Number 1" enemy, and throughout the war exerted himself to overthrow it. It required all of General Marshall's firmness and moderation to restrain him. The Navy, although the Pacific war was chiefly its responsibility and involved its pride, remained faithful to the principle that the European Axis must be defeated first. But Admiral King was impatient to see the Axis finished off so that the Navy could concentrate its whole force on Japan. Furthermore, when General MacArthur and the Navy were permitted in July 1942 to go over to limited offensives, and these were attended with success, it became very difficult not to reinforce them with troops and equipment that were not earmarked for decisive use in Europe. In July 1942, when decisive action in Europe seemed impossible to agree on and the reluctance of the British to agree to such action wore down the patience of the American Joint Chiefs, it required the President's intervention to prevent them from going all-out in the Pacific. The considered judgment of the American Joint Chiefs upheld Mr. Roosevelt.[20] But it did not make sense not to reinforce General MacArthur and Admiral Nimitz up to the margin of safety, and we did.

The Allied debate about OVERLORD was finally resolved in December 1943 at Tehran, in favor of the American view. General Eisenhower was appointed Supreme Commander. There was no more debate. With the all-out support of Churchill and the British Chiefs of Staff he amassed the powerful force that invaded France on June 6, 1944. Within a year it had knifed to the heart of Germany, met the Russians on the Elbe, and completed the work of utter destruction that the Soviet forces and the air bombing of Germany had begun.

[20] Matloff and Snell, *Strategic Planning*, pp. 267-273; for other references to the "Pacific Alternative," see pp. 161, 163, and 182.

The resolution of the long debate is commonly attributed to the emphatic judgment of Stalin delivered at Tehran that the contribution of the Western Allies in 1944 should not be further operations in the Mediterranean, for which Mr. Churchill was still pleading, but a power-drive against Germany from France, coordinated with one by the Russians from the East.

Stalin's intervention may have tipped the scale, as far as Mr. Churchill was concerned. But before deciding how much further persuasion the British needed, it is important to bear in mind a fact mentioned earlier: by mid-1943 the whole environment and atmosphere of Allied strategic planning had changed. The Allies had entered the second period of the war. They had emerged from a period of shortages into a period of sufficiency, if not of plenty. By the end of 1943 they had enough of everything, except landing craft, for operations of great magnitude.

In the first period the argument for a policy of opportunity had been hard indeed to resist. Thus the important decision for TORCH in July 1942 was based on a situation, not a theory. The principle followed was: "Here's what we have: what is the best we can do with it, if we are to use it in 1942?" The American Joint Chiefs were bitterly disappointed with the decision to expend it in a secondary theater. But their eagerness to get at the Germans in 1942 had not been in vain, since the BOLERO build-up had thrown into the British Isles the air and ground forces necessary for mounting TORCH.

The same principle of opportunism was followed in the decisions extending the Mediterranean campaign, first into Sicily, then into Italy, then up to Rome. Common sense, or perhaps wisdom, rather than strategic theory prevailed. Hitler having chosen, unwisely, to fight in Italy, instead of withdrawing his forces into a central reserve, it seemed only reasonable to keep the Germans pinned down in Italy and inflict on them a maximum of casualties.

But the Allies were now entering the second period of their joint enterprise, when the policy of concentration on a decisive blow made better sense, if the objective of unlimited war on Germany was not to be abandoned. Consequently, when Mr. Churchill moved heaven and earth to get more force thrown into Italy, at the same time resourcefully and vigorously contending for expeditions to seize islands in the Eastern Mediterranean and to threaten the Balkans, the Combined Chiefs of Staff, as well as General Eisenhower, firmly opposed him. I suggest that this was less the result of American rigidity than a result of a new logistical situation in which a policy of strategic opportunism seemed no longer either necessary or wise. The principle now was: "This is what we can do and are going to do by June 1, 1944, or Hitler may escape from defeat."

Such considerations raise the interesting question whether the most useful way to study strategic decisions is to concentrate on conflicting theories and plans. What was responsible for the kind of action taken? Was it the views of the planners of strategy or was it the force of circumstances operating at the moment of decision and the subsequent course of events and action of persons on whom the decisions were imposed? The answer history already can give us is that it was both, in various proportions.

The basic strategic decision regarding the war against Japan was that the Allies would give offensives against the European Axis first claim on the resources necessary to defeat their enemies. But what happened makes it a legitimate question whether we did not defeat the Japanese as quickly as we would have if our declared purpose had not been to beat Germany first. In the offensives which Admiral Nimitz and General MacArthur launched in the Pacific in 1943 and 1944, applying ground, air, and sea power in new and ingenious combinations, the limiting factors were carriers and land bases for aircraft, the seizure of which again depended on the recovery of the United States Fleet. The war in Europe did not materially delay our progress in building our new Navy, and until that new Navy, with its carriers and its floating repair and supply system was available, more ground combat troops could not be used, no matter how many could have been shipped and supplied.[21] My Pacific historians tell me that no major operation in the Pacific, regarded by the Allies as vital, was cancelled or seriously delayed for lack of troops or supplies. As soon as aircraft-

[21] This statement is subject to qualification by an "unless." The building of the new Navy and of the landing craft necessary to speed up the offensives against Japan could not have been achieved more promptly unless the President had been willing to increase still further and very substantially the allocation of steel and facilities for these purposes. But this would have meant not only postponing the defeat of Hitler but also risking the defeat of our European allies by him. In other words, it would have meant risking even the success of a holding action in Europe.

carriers, air bases, and shipping became available, the
Pacific offensives went forward with amazing speed. By
the end of 1943, two years after Pearl Harbor, MacArthur and Nimitz had projected their forces 1,300 miles
into the enemy's defenses. By the spring of 1945 they
had destroyed his shipping, crippled his fleet, and
planted their forces in positions from which we
cracked the heart of Japan three months after Hitler
had bitten the dust and before the forces liberated by
the defeat of Germany could be redeployed.

Perhaps the best indication that practical considerations and good sense prevailed over theory in deter-
mining the strategy of the Allies is that the final plan
for OVERLORD, their major combined offensive, embodied the strategic concepts for which both partners
had contended.[22] When they put it into effect they had
tightened the ring around the Axis almost to the point
of strangulation. The line through the Mediterranean
had been reopened and the lifeline between the two
great British spheres of power restored. The Allies had
knocked Italy out of the war. They had regained their
supremacy on the high seas; they had gained superiority in the air. They had kept Hitler's forces off balance.
His war industries were being bombed night and day;
the *Luftwaffe* had been broken and crippled until it
could no longer either protect these or support his
armies; and his armies had been dispersed, pinned
down and bled by concentric Russian and Allied attacks until he could no longer form an effective reserve
for counterattack. To this extent the concept of strat-

[22] This idea is ably developed in the paper by Dr. Gordon
Harrison referred to in Notes 12 and 19.

egy urged by the British had prevailed, with tremendous effect. The Allies had "closed the ring" until it was becoming a noose. But when OVERLORD came, it was no mop-up. It was the power play for which the Americans had always contended, and the Allies put behind it the force and weight needed to drive it to the heart of Germany.

What are the lessons taught by this recital? They seem to be as follows:

Once a nation or coalition has decided on its basic objectives in war, three things are more important than the particular strategic plans that its planners make. One is that these plans embody timely and farsighted provision for the means necessary to achieve their basic objectives. The Nazis and the Japanese both failed for want of such foresight. The second is that a power or coalition must be ready to pass from short-range to long-range plans at the earliest possible date. The third is consistency in planning and execution. The fundamental fact that must be faced is that the build-up and execution of a large-scale offensive is too complex to allow for any substantial changes in a strategic plan without incurring critical delays and dangerously impairing morale.

Strategy is shaped on the anvil of necessity rather than by the plans of strategists. But in World War II one of the forces that hammered the strategy of the Allies into the effective shape that it took was the consistently and persistently offensive spirit of America's political and military chiefs, expressing itself in the conviction that only direct and powerful body-blows, delivered promptly, can break the will of a resourceful enemy.

IV

THE ARMY RE-SHAPED

WHAT WERE the means applied by the United States in World War II to attain its strategic objectives, as far as its Army was concerned? What was the shape of the military fist which it applied to the destruction of the power of Germany and Japan in 1944-1945? Consideration of this question must include the air arm, though the discussion that follows will be focused on the ground arms and services.

Necessity shaped the Army, as well as its strategy. And it happens that 1943 was the year in which the size, shape, and composition of our military forces, as well as the strategic plan of the Allies, were determined.

In the Victory Program racked up in the fall of 1941 the War Department had estimated that to defeat the Axis and Japan it must mobilize and arm a force of about 8,800,000 men.[1] That force was to include an air arm of unprecedented size and power. An Army Supply Program, based on the requirements of an army of this size, was geared into the industrial economy of the nation. That economy was then rapidly mobilized and retooled to produce the arms and supplies for such a force and at the same time for those that would have to be transferred to our Allies and Russia, to execute

[1] Matloff and Snell, *Strategic Planning for Coalition Warfare, 1941-1943*, p. 59.

the decision that the United States was both to fight and serve as "the Arsenal of Democracy."

In the summer of 1940 the Army had had an actual strength of less than 280,000 organized in scattered and incomplete units. It was anticipated that the new force of 8,800,000, called for by the Victory Program, would be shaped into a ground army of 215 divisions and an air force of 84 groups. By January 1, 1943 the War Department had brought into being partially equipped 73 divisions and 167 air combat groups. Seventeen divisions and 66 air groups had by that date been sent overseas.[2] Then came the year in which all previous decisions about the size and shape of the Army had to be recast.

To explain these decisions it will be helpful to recall certain elementary features of military organization.[3] The basic fact is that the military forces of the United States, like all others, consist of three primary elements: command and staff; arms and services; and the field forces. The staff plans. The commander, aided by a headquarters staff, decides and directs. The arms and services develop the specialties required in war. Examples of arms are Infantry, Artillery, the Air Corps. Examples of services are the Quartermaster Corps and the Ordnance Department. The combatant field forces fight. They are a vast team of tactical units, which the arms develop, which the services equip and

[2] *Ibid.,* pp. 350, 359.

[3] Parts of what follows appeared in an article by the author entitled "Forging the U. S. Army in World War II into a Combined Arms Team," published in the *Mississippi Valley Historical Review,* XXXVII, pp. 443-52. They are reproduced here with the courteous permission of the *Review.*

supply, and which commanders train for war and command in combat. In ground combat the largest permanent tactical unit of combined arms and services is the division. It is composed of units of several arms and services, combined in a proportion designed to enable it to fight on its own for a limited time under conditions estimated as normal in war.

In 1940, just when mobilization was beginning, the whole question of what kind of army the United States should have had been thrown into debate by the overwhelming successes of the German Army, followed by the bombing of England. The basic influence requiring fresh decisions was modern technology. The vast apparatus of machines necessary to win wars requires a high degree of specialization. The Army had to resolve the basic question of organization that faced, and faces, modern man: where and how strike the balance between specialization and effective teamwork?

The pressure for specialization naturally showed up in the arms and services. The services had a staggering array of weapons and apparatus to procure and handle. The old arms were being mechanized and motorized. New arms were developing around power-driven military mechanisms: the tank, the tank destroyer, the war plane. The War Department had to decide how best to team the parent organizations, the arms and services, and also how to combine in the field the forces that these were putting forth for use against the enemy.

Two basic changes in the organization of the military establishment that profoundly affected its shape and the balance of forces within it were made in 1941-42. All of the services were swept together under a huge single continental command, the Army Service Forces, and all but one of the arms were integrated into another, the Army Ground Forces. The exception in the case of the arms was of great importance. The air arm, in June 1941, had been raised to the level of a force, and endowed with a staff and services of its own. In March 1942 the Army Air Forces, thus called into being, was made coordinate with the Army Ground Forces and the Army Service Forces.[4] In the new Army of the United States taking shape in 1941 the air arm became the largest, as well as the most richly endowed, of the combat arms.

The pressure for technical specialization showed up also in the shape that the field forces were taking. Specialization went fastest and farthest in the new Air Forces. But in 1940-42 a rush in the same direction swept through the ground forces. With eagerness to extract a maximum of mobility and striking power from machines and motors came a surge toward special types of large permanent units: motorized divisions, airborne divisions, heavy armored divisions, armored corps, and even armored armies. The swing towards specialization called even for mountain divi-

[4] These changes were incidental to a sweeping reorganization of the War Department that went into effect on March 9, 1942. The most detailed history of this reorganization is in F. Stansbury Haydon, "War Department Reorganization, August 1941-March 1942," Part I, *Military Affairs* (Spring 1952), Vol. XVI, No. 1, pp. 12-29; Part II (Fall 1952), Vol. XVI, No. 3, pp. 97-114. This account is supplemented by John D. Millett, *Organization and Role of the Army Service Forces* (a forthcoming volume in *United States Army in World War II)*, Chaps. I and II.

sions and jungle divisions. All of these required specialized and elaborate equipment.[5]

The United States approached and entered World War II with a traditional confidence that its resources for waging war were unlimited. The heavily mechanized ground and air forces which we undertook to mobilize, send overseas, and maintain in far-away places, plus the demands to be met by us as "the Arsenal" of the other fighting "democracies," threw a fantastic burden on our productive capacity. By the fall of 1942, after a year of plunging expansion, strain, and stress, we came squarely up against the exceedingly unpleasant fact that the production and mobilization goals for 1942, and even more those for 1943, were beyond the limits of feasibility. The whole military program of the United States would have to be cut back. Where and how were the cuts to be made?

The allocation both of productive capacity and of manpower had to be overhauled. The President made the basic decisions. He decided that "foreign aid to arm the trained manpower of other anti-Axis nations" was not to be heavily cut. Within our own forces, the air program was to be the one most lightly cut. The shipbuilding program was upped, since it was useless to mobilize, arm, and train forces that could not be shipped and supplied. "The production program that emerged by the end of 1942 had a definite emphasis

5 K. R. Greenfield, Robert R. Palmer, and Bell I. Wiley, *Organization of Ground Combat Troops* (Washington, 1947), pp. 56-98, 277-78, 325-26, 336-50, *United States Army in World War II.*

and a definite shape. The main emphasis was to be on air power."[6]

It is not difficult to understand the decision to continue to give the Air Forces preferential treatment. If the United States was to strike the enemy in Europe promptly, it would have to strike first through the air. In any case, economy of force required that air superiority be achieved in all theaters at the earliest possible date. A strong element in the Air Forces believed they could knock out the enemy with very little help on the ground. The Army Air Forces, given the right of way, proceeded to concentrate on its build-up for a combined, Anglo-American bomber offensive against Germany that might smash the nerve-centers of Hitler's power and prove the case for strategic bombing.

The brunt of economy and reorganization, therefore, fell on the ground and service forces. Their problem could not be met by increasing their size, for the manpower crisis that confronted the Army in the winter of 1942-43 was national. We waked up to the unpleasant fact that, in spite of the efficiency of our labor force, the American nation simply did not have the manpower to keep its own economy going and to carry out besides all the war tasks we had undertaken.

[6] Leighton and Coakley, *Logistics of Global Warfare, 1941-1943* (forthcoming volume in *United States Army in World War II*), Chap. XXII. Their tabulation shows the following changes made in October 1942 after review by the Joint Chiefs of Staff:

AIR PROGRAM: cut 10% (to produce 109,000 aircraft).

ARMY GROUND FORCE PROGRAM: cut 21% (for a ground Army of 3,130,000 enlisted men).

NAVY PROGRAM: cut 17.8%

SHIPBUILDING PROGRAM: upped 22%

The President decided that the Army had to accept a total of 7,700,000 enlisted men (about 8,200,000, counting officers) as the ceiling on its share of American manpower.[7] It was now going to be necessary for the War Department to apply strict priorities to the distribution of this slice among its forces.

To those who regarded a massive, hard-hitting ground army as necessary to achieve our strategic aims this was a disconcerting conclusion. For the War Department had already learned that it had grossly underestimated the proportion of its forces that would have to be service troops.

The War Department had tended to fix its thought on service troops organic to its combat forces. But during 1942 other requirements for service units that could not be avoided mounted into alarming figures.

Engineer, Signal, Quartermaster, Ordnance, Medical, Chemical Warfare, Transportation services and a bewildering variety of units of specialized types within each service—such as: port battalions, railroad units, heavy ponton battalions, engineer amphibious brigades, truck companies, dump truck companies, laundry companies, decontamination companies, smoke generator companies, station and field hospitals, graves registration units, to mention only a few—were demanded by every new base and theater. They were needed to build and repair roads, bridges, and fuel lines, establish and operate communications by wire and radio (including a world-wide network), recon-

[7] Robert R. Palmer, "Ground Forces in the Army, Dec. 1941-April 1945: a Statistical Study," in Greenfield, Palmer, and Wiley, *Organization,* pp. 159-84.

struct and operate seaports, build airbases, warehouses, and cantonments, keep guns, tanks, and trucks in repair, keep the Army in health and care for its sick, wounded and dead, and, finally, to keep rolling ever-increasing streams of supply from one port, depot and base to another, through "pipelines" of ships, railroads, trucks, and air transports, warehouses, depots, and supply dumps, to reach the combat forces on time, and in the right quantities and proportions—all this and more, not to a single theater, as in World War I, but all over the globe in every variety of terrain and climate. To these organizations must be added the numerous units and headquarters of the "administrative services," such as the Adjutant General, the Provost Marshal General and his Military Police, and the Finance Corps, which performed the "housekeeping" functions of the Army.

The Army had not only to supply and keep house for its own community of 8,000,000. On its shoulders fell also the enormous task of administering Lend-Lease to our Allies. And then, after a discouraging attempt in North Africa to have civilian agencies of the Government administer civil affairs and supply the civilian population of an occupied area, it became evident that the Army would also have to take over both of these burdens, and it did, for the duration of the war.[8]

Add up all of these administrative demands and there begins to emerge some notion of the claim that

[8] This process is traced in Albert K. Weinberg and Harry L. Coles, *Soldiers Become Governors,* a forthcoming volume in *United States Army in World War II.*

the Army's need for services at home and in a multi-theater war put on its share of the nation's manpower.

During 1942 the Army had had to build up four theaters for its own operations, demanding all such services: one in Australia, over 6,000 miles away; one based on New Caledonia in the South Pacific; one in England, for the bombing of Germany and the proposed invasion of the Continent; then, suddenly in the fall of 1942, another in North Africa, to support the occupation of Morocco and Algeria and the conquest of Tunisia. During 1942 the Army, in addition, had to create two theaters, complete with service troops, to support the forces of other nations fighting against our enemies. One was the Middle East Theater based on Cairo. This was at first designed to support the British in Egypt and Mesopotamia. But in 1942 the Army also had to take over and finish in this theater the task of operating "the Persian Corridor," reaching from the head of the Persian Gulf to Tehran, the purpose of which was to deliver the bulk of our aid to Russia, when the cruel Arctic route to Archangel and Murmansk had to be shut down. The other, even more fabulous service theater which began to absorb Army strength in 1942 was the China-Burma-India Theater. It stretched from Karachi on the West Coast of India to Kunming in Southwest China—approximately the distance from Sacramento, California, to Washington, D. C. Its two missions were to equip Chiang Kai-shek to keep his nation at war with Japan after the Burma Road was cut, and eventually to establish air bases in China from which the Army Air Forces could bomb the Japanese homeland. Our only combat forces in this vast theater were its famous commander General Joseph Stilwell, one regiment of infantry ("Merrill's Marauders") , and air forces. But China-Burma-India eventually absorbed more than 150,000 American service troops. By 1944 the Persian Corridor was employing 27,000 of them.[9]

To sum up, the Army in 1942 was taking a shape imposed by the emphasis on air power and by a demand not clearly foreseen—"the demand for shipping, personnel and overhead created by supplies which included a mass of heavy and complicated mechanical equipment" and the task of stocking these in scattered and distant theaters. The bulk of these supplies was increased, it must be added, by "the pressure to enable American soldiers to take their standard of living with them."[10] The striking force that the United States could deliver in combat was going to depend on its combat efficiency and the degree to which the size of its administrative forces could be limited without impairing that efficiency.

In the last months of 1942 General Marshall, caught between a manpower ceiling and an apparently incompressible demand for service troops, made a decision that was momentous in its effect on the composition of the Army. He decided that the necessary sav-

[9] Strength Report of the Army, July 31, 1941. For the history of the "service theaters" mentioned, see T. H. Vail Motter, *The Persian Corridor and Aid to Russia* (Washington, 1952) and the three volumes devoted to China-Burma-India, by Chares F. Romanus and Riley Sunderand, of which the first has been published: *Stilwell's Mission to China* (Washington, 1953)—all in *United States Army in World War II.*

[10] Palmer, in *Organization*, p. 258.

ings in the Army's manpower must be made in its ground combat forces. In the spring of 1943 he slowed down the activation of divisions, pending the outcome of the Allied bomber offensive against Germany and of the offensive that the Russians were launching as they rebounded from the agony of Stalingrad. In the summer of 1943 he decided to suspend the creation of more divisions, and no more were activated. As a result the Army had only 89 divisions with which to finish the war on the ground in all theaters, instead of the 215 originally estimated as necessary.

Meanwhile the War Department had adopted a sweeping reorganization of both the ground and air forces.

The reorganization of the Army Ground Forces was carried out with zest by their brilliant and sardonic commander, Lt. General Lesley J. McNair.[11] He passed their organization through a wringer at his headquarters, the Reduction Board, determined to squeeze from every part of it what he regarded as fat, and General McNair, a Scotsman, had very strict notions of economy. By "fat" General McNair meant every person or piece of equipment in a unit which did not contribute directly to its fighting power and which it did not need at all times to accomplish its mission. He was convinced that he could at the same time increase the mobility and striking power of his forces by applying the principles of pooling and more flexible control.

[11] This reorganization is analyzed in a masterly study by Palmer, *ibid*, pp. 261-382, on which this and the following paragraphs are based.

When the ground forces came out of his wringer, their organization was both simpler and leaner. The motorized division and all other specialized types of infantry division had disappeared, except five airborne divisions and one mountain division. Armored corps vanished. The proportion of armored to infantry was cut down. From each infantry division 1,261 men and about 20 per cent of its vehicles had been taken; from each armored division 3,683 men and 127 tanks. All nondivisional units, such as tank battalions, had been similarly pared down. The size of headquarters, especially higher headquarters, was attacked, since General McNair was convinced that they established (to quote him) "a mass of ritual and paperwork" and unnecessary coordination which threatened to block the rapidity of action for which modern armies were physically equipped. He believed that headquarters, like units, ought to be so organized as to maximize the use of each person.

The men and equipment saved were organized into smaller units of specialized types, generally of battalion size, as for example, tank battalions. These were to be controlled by small "group" headquarters. To achieve economy of force, and to permit the massing of power when and where needed, smaller units were to be combined with each other or with divisions to form forces tailor-made to carry out given military tasks.

In short, specialized nondivisional units were pooled. The principle applied was to push as far back and up the ladder of command as practicable all resources, whether in motor transport, supporting firepower, or special types of units, not normally and instantly needed at the point of contact with the enemy, instead of leaving them in fixed combinations where they would be unemployed much of the time. They could be then thrown into action by higher headquarters, corps, or army, whenever the need was critical.

This concept of "task forces" and "reinforced combat teams" was nothing new in 1942-43. What was new was the vigor with which General McNair and General Marshall now applied it, convinced that the existing organization of American ground forces failed to take full advantage of the speed of movement which the combustion engine and electric and radio communication, if properly exploited in war, would permit. On the other hand, General McNair, in reducing the heavy mechanized equipment of his units, argued that mechanization had reached the point where it was impeding mobility. He believed that ground forces must travel light to travel fast. He also took seriously the injunction given him by the War Department on October 25, 1942 that in view of the then critical shortage of shipping "the trend must be toward light, easily transportable units."

The Army Air Forces also underwent a reorganization in 1943. As in the ground forces the principle of pooling was applied, but here more drastically because of the greater mobility of air forces. The result was greater tactical elasticity. On the other hand, the reorganization of the air forces was not governed by the regard for economy of means which General McNair felt it necessary and proper to observe.

The manpower crisis of 1943 brought the service

forces as well as the ground forces under heavy pressure to economize. They undertook it with the whip of their forceful chief, General Brehon B. Somervell, cracking over them. The services, and also the combat forces, were required to substitute limited service troops, women in uniform (WAC's), civilians, and eventually prisoners of war, in rear areas and noncombat functions, for troops who could fight. General Somervell also exerted himself, with conspicuous success, to rationalize and consolidate his world-wide system of supply, once the wasteful rush of 1942 and early 1943 was over, and strategic plans became firmer.[12] But the appetite of the Army's huge and far-flung service establishment for more and more service troops was insatiable, and ate up much of the Army manpower saved by the reduction and streamlining of the combat ground forces.

A few figures will illustrate the effect on the ultimate shape of the Army of the United States in World War II. The peak strength of the Medical Department alone (world-wide) was considerably more than 600,000. It therefore embraced a force three times as large as the whole Regular Army in 1939; larger than the Army of the Confederacy in the Civil War; and had four times the strength of the forces on both sides in the battle of Gettysburg. By July 31, 1944 there were 677,217 troops in the Corps of Engineers; over 500,000 in the Quartermaster Corps; over a million in the other four technical services.[13]

[12] Millett, *Army Service Forces,* Chap. XXIII; Leighton and Coakley, *Logistics 1941-1943,* Chapter XXIII.
[13] "Summary of Conclusions to Date," prepared for the author

The shape of our World War II Army showed, besides service elements, another growth that was unanticipated and that was not brought under control. This was the expansion and "proliferation of overhead" in the form of higher headquarters. These headquarters ate up officers needed for leadership in combat and tended to confuse the chain of command. General McNair kept his own headquarters lean with only 270 commissioned officers (and 964 other persons) in it at the end of 1943. But the Washington headquarters of the Army Air Forces at the same time included 685 officers (and over 3,000 others) and Headquarters, Army Service Forces, in Washington had reached the enormous total of 7,227 commissioned officers and 39,247 other persons.[14] All efforts to resist this top-heavy growth and to work with lean headquarters were in vain. A proclivity to handle each new function by assigning another person or another office to perform it, not unknown to American civilian practice, probably played its part in the proliferation of man-eating overhead, but the tendency was rooted in the requirements of modern warfare. The multiplication of specialties in war, as in civil life, increases the need for coordination. A headquarters staff is the technical brain of the commander, and the direction of complex forces calls for a big multicellular brain. The principle of pooling, applied to both ground and air

by Dr. Donald O. Wagner, Chief Historian of the Army Medical Service, March 22, 1953; Strength Reports of the Army (STM-30), July 31, 1944.

14 From Table prepared by the Statistics Branch, General Staff, January 17, 1944, OCMH Files.

forces, threw heavier and more complex duties on higher headquarters in the field. In field forces of the ground army the Victory Program forecast a need for 215 divisions directed by 5 field armies. But we wound up with 10 field army headquarters directing only 89 divisions. At the very top, coordination with the British had to be organized and this produced such vast organizations as Allied Force Headquarters in the Mediterranean, with a strength of 3,072 at the end of 1943, and Supreme Headquarters, Allied Expeditionary Forces, with 1,810 commissioned officers and a total personnel of 16,312 at the beginning of 1945.[15] The gibe was current during the war that the American Army was "all headquarters and no hindquarters."

The Army that emerged to fight the decisive battles of 1944 had a long-reaching, heavy, and powerful air fist. It had a comparatively small and compact ground fist. In 1945 only about 30 per cent of our air and ground forces combined were in combatant units.[16] The rest were engaged in "overhead" operations or in services of supply.

In our Army as it finally shaped up, not only were the ground forces in smaller proportion and its large ground force units more lightly equipped than had been intended originally, but its ground combat soldiers were inferior to those in the air and service forces in the qualities measured by the Army's military

[15] (1) "History of AFHQ," Part II, Sec. 1, p. 246 (OCMH Files); (2) Appendix "SHAEF Personnel," in Forrest C. Pogue, *The Supreme Command,* a forthcoming volume in *United States Army in World War II.*

[16] Greenfield, Palmer, and Wiley, *Organization,* p. 170.

aptitude tests. This inferiority was partly the result of the popularity of air service with young Americans and the methods by which the preferential treatment deliberately accorded the Air Forces in 1942 and 1943 allowed the Army Air Forces to turn this popularity to their advantage in recruiting high-grade men. But the relatively inferior quality of the ground combat troops also is traceable to the unanticipated effect produced by the Army's carefully studied system of classification and assignment.[17]

The Army's classification system was designed to effect an economy of training effort in the rapid mass production of a civilian army. It sought this result by typing and assigning largely on the basis of civilian skills. But while specific in regard to technical specialties useful in war, it contained only general tests and specifications for the qualities that make a good leader or an effective fighter. The unforeseen effect of the system on distribution of high-grade manpower within the Army was determined by the American emphasis on vocationalism, at the expense of the all-round man, for young Americans who had already acquired technical and mechanical skills were the very ones likely to have the background, resourcefulness, and aptitude for leadership and success in battle. The Army's classification system tended to throw these men into technical assignments and the military services in which technical specialties were concentrated, that is, into the air

17 Robert R. Palmer, "The Procurement of Enlisted Personnel: the Problem of Quality," in Palmer, Wiley, and Keast, *The Procurement and Training of Ground Combat Troops*, pp. 1-86, *United States Army in World War II.*

and service forces rather than into the ground combat army. The discrepancy, particularly as it affected the Infantry, became so alarming that in 1944 the classi-fication system was modified by introducing the so-called Physical Profile. This emphasized personal rug-gedness and gave the ground forces first call on men possessing it. The "Profile" came to stay. But during World War II, for various reasons, it produced no great effect. The only measures that contributed sub-stantially to redressing the balance were the assign-ment to the ground forces of most of the collegians in the Army Specialist Training Program when that was cut back in February, 1944, and block-transfers to the Army Ground Forces of high-grade men from the air and service forces later in that year when the need for infantry replacements became critical.

Again, the fist of ground forces with which the Army dealt its blows at the enemy was not as well trained as its plans required, in spite of the early mobilization of the American Army, and the period of grace af-forded by the preoccupation of Hitler's armies with the Russians.[18]

In World War I its divisions had had to be thrown into battle with only the sketchiest training, and a number of them had to be broken up into kindling wood at home and in France to provide replacements. The Army, mindful of this experience, established two goals in preparing itself for World War II. One was to weld its divisions and other units into genuine bat-tle teams before they were committed to battle. The

18 *Ibid.*, especially pp. 429-63 (Bell I. Wiley, "The Building and Training of Infantry Divisions").

other was to provide a sufficiency of well-trained filler replacements. Neither ideal was realized.

The ideal of welding divisions into genuine battle teams was to be achieved by having them pass through carefully planned stages of training, culminating in field maneuvers with all their supporting elements. This training, made as realistic as possible, was to be accomplished while they were still in the United States, leaving only training and rehearsals for particular situations to be given them overseas. It was, and is, an article of faith in the Army that team spirit, the pride of a soldier in his unit, willingness to do and endure heightened by association with men with whom one has learned to work, is vital to the battle effectiveness of a civilian army, and that this can be attained only by continuous association of the officers and men of a unit through training into battle. The strict correlation between habits and comradeship and the effectiveness of American ground troops in battle was fully confirmed by experience in World War II.[19] But in the ground forces, particularly in the Infantry, such association proved to be impossible of attainment. Only the divisions trained and shipped overseas before 1943—fourteen in number—were products of the full training program. The remaining seventy-three trained in the United States were, when sent overseas, far from being thoroughly trained and integrated battle teams.

Of all the interferences and setbacks that disorganized divisional training, the most serious in the

[19] S.L.A. Marshall, *Men Against Fire*, Washington, 1947.

long run was the incidence of casualties in the infantry elements of divisions fighting in Europe.[20] This repeatedly exceeded calculations made in advance. Unanticipated losses were reflected in a rising demand for replacements, and in sudden peaks in this demand, as for example, in the fall and winter of 1944. These could be met only by stripping divisions still in training. These, except airborne divisions, were repeatedly stripped and refilled until in their infantry elements, the foundation of the divisional team, they resembled the sock imagined by eighteenth-century wits that was darned so often that nothing of the original was left but the shape. The effect on the divisions in battle was the same. Because their number was so small those in Europe had to be kept continuously in the line. The incidence of casualties concentrated on these few divisions produced some staggering figures. "During intensive combat an infantry division suffered about 100 per cent losses in its infantry regiments every three months." Since fresh divisions were not available, these losses were made good by individual replacements and these generally had to be assimilated while the division was fighting.

Under such circumstances most of our divisions committed to battle were not firmly welded teams in the desired and desirable sense, and a large proportion of the replacements poured into them, while they had received some small-unit training, had never been members of a well-integrated battle team.

[20] Robert R. Palmer, "The Provision of Enlisted Replacements," in Palmer, Wiley, and Keast, *Procurement and Training,* pp. 169-239.

"The battle is the pay-off."

That is the point to which the study of military preparations and military systems must always return for perspective. What can be said, as of now, of the American Army's performance in battle? The history of battle as fought by Americans on the ground, in the air, and on the sea in World War II, although it has been written with unprecedented speed, is still incomplete. The returns are not all in. But on the basis of incomplete returns, certain observations legitimately can be made.

In the foregoing exposition much has been said of disappointments. But the Army in question was a victorious Army. Only once, at the very beginning, in the Philippines, was it forced to execute a great retrograde movement ending in surrender. But that movement was distinguished by a tactical skill and a resourcefulness and heroism in the face of overwhelming odds that made the withdrawal to Bataan and the fighting there one of the brightest and most honorable pages in the history of American arms and the Philippine nation. Once, and only once, in the Ardennes, in December 1944, was the American Army set back on its haunches, but it rallied at once and snatched a smashing victory from the jaws of defeat.[21]

Moving from victory to victory, the Army turned in a remarkable record of mobility. Only four times was it reduced to anything resembling the dreaded static

[21] Louis Morton, *The Fall of the Philippines,* Washington, 1953, *United States Army in World War II.* The volume in that series on the battle of "the Bulge" by Hugh M. Cole is nearing completion.

trench-warfare of World War I: in Italy in the winter of 1943-44 at Cassino and again in the winter of 1944-45 at the foot of the Apennines; in Northwest Europe for a moment in July 1944 in the hedgerow country of Normandy, and then in the Siegfried Line in the dark fall and the darker December of that year. For the rest, our forces moved forward with astonishing speed across the face of Europe and across the vast reaches of the Pacific. From 1943 on our air forces advanced swiftly and without a serious check to mastery of the air over the battle areas and then over the homelands of the enemy.

The Army that achieved this record was a motorized force and one heavily armed with the devices of a mechanized civilization. Unable to go as far as it hoped in this direction, the War Department threw the chief weight of the Army's mechanized effort into its air forces, applying a relative economy to others. Nevertheless, we counted heavily on motor transport and mechanical force. Let us, then, look for a moment at the record of the Army's combinations, or teams of arms, designed to make the most of the mechanisms of war.

The record leaves little doubt that the most efficient of these combinations was the infantry-artillery team. This team was built into the division; indeed the infantry division of World War II was primarily an infantry-artillery team. Divisional artillery, reinforced with a mass of corps and army artillery, was often the giant member of the team and performed the decisive role in battle—a fact easily overlooked because modern military narration, like all tales of battle from time immemorial, tends to focus on men in motion. The enemy knew. From both sides of the world he has testified again and again, with astonishment and dismay, to the accurate and overwhelming fires with which American artillery isolated and pulverized his positions and stunned and decimated his forces. In many decisive engagements the role of the infantry was not to break through but to occupy and mop up positions in which artillery concentrations had shattered the power of the foe.[22] American artillery did not owe this deadly effectiveness to its weapons, which were in some respects inferior to those of the Germans, but to the skill with which American artillery was used, the accuracy with which it could pin-point its fires, and the techniques it had developed to shift and mass them. The fact that most impressed our foes was the speed and accuracy with which concentrations of artillery fire could be brought down on a target at the request of even a company commander, thanks to the efficiency of our system of communication and fire control.

Armored forces were newcomers in the American Army of World War II. Tankmen and infantrymen gradually learned to work together. But the two arms did not work into an intimate partnership like that

[22] An interesting example of the persistence of the Infantry point of view occurs in *Three Battles* (Washington, 1952, *United States Army in World War II*), p. 103, where Sidney T. Mathews, on the first page of his fine study of "The Break-Through at Monte Altuzzo," refers to the small infantry force engaged (never more than two companies) as "the fist" of the attack, whereas his study clearly shows that the enormous artillery fire laid on the Giogo Pass was the fist of steel that broke the German line.

of infantry and artillery, except in the armored division. The American Armored Force inherited the traditions and outlook of the Cavalry. Both Infantry and Armor had to learn how dependent tanks were on infantry except in situations that were unusual in World War II. They had to learn that it was necessary for the infantry-artillery team to pry a hole through the enemy's lines before the tanks could break through and race away shooting. This lesson was disappointing to the doughboys, humiliating to cavalry-minded tankers, and hard to learn. Under the pooling system, the normal practice was to reinforce an infantry division by attaching to it a tank battalion when needed. Battalions which could be repeatedly teamed up with the same divisions learned to work effectively with them. After the war a tank battalion was made an organic part of each infantry division.

Although the teaming with infantry essential to the best use of armor was not perfected during the war, American armor more than paid off, especially in Europe, in sharpening the cutting edge of tactical offensives, and pushing American firepower rapidly into the enemy's rear, and beyond, wherever weakness in his line was found or created; in short, in keeping the battle fluid. Its effectiveness, like that of our artillery, was due to the skill with which it was used. Our tanks were outgunned and outweighed by certain types employed by the Germans. But they outnumbered and outran German tanks, thanks to the ingenious offensiveness with which they were employed by commanders like Patton; thanks also to their superior mechanical dependability, and thanks also, in all probability, to the aptitude of American youngsters for operating, humoring, and patching up machinery.

The air and ground forces of the Army of the United States did not develop an effective air-ground battle team in World War II. The Marines did, in cooperation with naval aviation and their own. The Army Air Forces were too much preoccupied with other interests and goals: with strategic bombing; with freedom from entangling alliances, in order to protect the precious flexibility of their forces and permit shifting them quickly; with independence of any control but their own, except at theater level. Close-in support of the ground forces was one of their missions, but the one given lowest priority. It was impossible to interest them seriously in developing the equipment, techniques or skills needed for genuine teamwork in ground combat.[23]

But lift your sights to the level at which the Army air forces operated as the co-equal of the Army ground forces and the picture changes completely. At that level they were the most effective partner that the Army ground forces had except the armies of the USSR. Gaining the mastery of the air over the Mediterranean after a hard struggle in early 1943, the Army Air Forces, teamed with the Royal Air Force, drove Goering's great *Luftwaffe* from the skies over the battlefields of the continent. Without them the invasion of Normandy in June 1944 would have been impos-

[23] The difficulties of the Army Ground Forces in obtaining effective cooperation from the Army Air Forces are set forth in Kent Roberts Greenfield, *Army Ground Forces and the Air-Ground Battle Team,* Study No. 35 in the series prepared by the Historical Section, AGF, reproduced in lithotype, 1948.

sible. They raised a vast air umbrella over it; isolated the whole lodgment area; crippled the forces the Germans tried to assemble for counterattack; helped to blast the opening at St Lô through which the First and Third U. S. Armies broke into the open on July 25 and began to race across France; then smashed the Nazi formations that Patton and Hodges rounded up as they raced. Meanwhile, the Allied air forces systematically destroyed the sources of fuel oil in Germany, crippling the mobility of the German armies.

In the Southwest Pacific at this same level Army Ground and Air Forces, under General MacArthur and General Kenney, worked out an even more remarkable partnership. There the objects of the two were intertwined. The object of the ground forces was to move as rapidly, and in as long leaps, as possible, from island to island, base to base, with the ultimate objective of invading Japan. They needed the air force to accomplish these moves. But each new base occupied by the Army provided a landing field and airdrome from which the air force could leap forward until it was within bombing distance of the Japanese homeland. When General MacArthur's forces from the Southwest Pacific and Admiral Nimitz's from the Central Pacific converged and their combined forces had taken the Philippines and Okinawa, both objectives had been achieved. Hurling the B-29's of its XX Bomber Command from the Marianas and Okinawa to blast and burn the cities of Japan and finally to drop the atom bomb, it was the Army Air Forces that gave the last turn of the screw which brought the Japanese Empire to its knees.

V

SOME GENERAL OBSERVATIONS

THE PHENOMENON of success achieved by the Army that emerges from the foregoing pages still seems little short of miraculous. An Army and Air Force that contained less than 15,000 officers and 250,000 enlisted men in 1940 expanded by 1945 to a force of more than 8,000,000, very few of whom had been previously trained for war. The War Department insisted on a strategy based on power-drives: the one executed in 1944-45 in Europe, and the one for which the United States was concentrating its forces in the Pacific when the Japanese surrendered in August 1945. American forces were largely, in the case of the Pacific almost entirely, responsible for executing these drives. In spite of the fact that, contrary to plan, all but 30 per cent of the Army's strength, on the ground and in the air, had to go into supporting services, that 30 per cent executed its missions victoriously.

As of now, it can safely be said that the Army's success could not have been achieved when it was, if at all, had not the enormous mass of Russian troops thrown against the German armies pinned the bulk of these to the eastern front in Europe. This gave us time to mobilize. It created a global balance of ground strength which the Allies could tilt against Germany with decisive success, while the United States was sending to the Pacific the ground forces necessary to support the drive of its naval and air forces against the Japanese. The successes achieved would hardly have been possible without the enormous weight of machines, munitions, and ships that American industry proved capable of turning out in record time. Finally, we could not have succeeded with the kind of ground army we produced but for the weight that we put into our air forces and the effectiveness with which it was applied. In the final clutch we had a ground force in Europe that barely sufficed. In May 1945 we had only two divisions that had never been committed to action —the 13th Airborne Division in Europe and the 98th Infantry Division in Hawaii. General Marshall has referred to this photofinish as vindicating the accuracy of our calculation of the force we would need to defeat the Axis.[1] But it also means that we finished the war in Europe with virtually no reserve of ground combat forces ready and available for action.

In the final equation the effectiveness with which our forces were employed in battle still seems a kind of miracle. How could the tiny professional nucleus of Army officers of 1939-40, with so little experience of war, and a miniature cadre of experienced troops under their command, develop a force that displayed such striking military effectiveness?

The final answer must be sought in many directions and the search would, of course, have to include such nonmilitary areas as the mechanical resourcefulness, the educability, the character and spirit of the nation.

[1] Biennial Report of The Chief of Staff, July 1, 1943 to June 30, 1945, to the Sec. of War, pp. 106-107.

It is too soon to say to what extent it is to be found in
the relative weight, skill, and spirit of the enemy's
resistance. One military factor that can easily be overlooked or underestimated has increasingly impressed
itself on all of our authors who are studying the
Army's campaigns in World War II. This is that, whatever changes took place in the shape of our forces
during their participation in the war, the doctrines
underlying their organization and tactical employment
did not change. We modified our tactics and adjusted
our organization to meet special conditions. Conditions in the jungles of Pacific islands and those in the
Mediterranean or Normandy were, of course, different
and we varied the combinations and employment of
our forces to meet them. But the infantry division as
organized in 1941 proved effective as the basic combat
unit, our weapons were much the same and similarly
employed throughout the war and in all theaters, and
the ways in which American commanders and their
troops had learned to use their formations and equipment proved to be effective everywhere. The changes
and modifications were not as basic as they may at
first seem, and, as observed above, those made in 1943
were in the nature of a return to first principles. Our
authors are coming to the conclusion that if the doctrines with which the Army applied itself to its enormous task in 1940-41 were not substantially changed
during the war, it was because they did not need to be
changed. They are persuaded that the report repeatedly made by our commanders during the war: "Our
doctrines are sound" (made with evident satisfaction,

but with overtones of relief if not surprise) is confirmed by the record of performance.

The credit for this goes to the Army's schools and to the type of officers that the Army was able to attract between the first and second world wars. In those schools these officers worked out and absorbed the doctrines that stood the test of war. With an imagination and a professional dedication beyond all praise they performed this great task of preparation in a period when the Army was kept lean to the point of emaciation by the indifference, not to say the fear and dislike, of the American people. Thanks to their dedication and the rigorous, thorough, and realistic training given in these schools, the nation possessed in its hour of danger not only a sound and elastic system of military organization and doctrine, but military leaders who, with little experience in the field beyond the peacetime command of small units, quickly rose to the command and staffing of divisions, corps, armies, and army groups and exercised it, in many cases, with brilliance. A conspicuous but representative example is General Eisenhower, who, not having commanded before 1942 a unit larger than a peacetime regiment, two years later successfully exercised operational control of the vast Allied forces that broke through the Siegfried Line, crossed the Rhine, and defeated the Germans in the West.

One further observation about the Army that is of general public interest seems to be justified in the light of the changes during the war in the general shape and relative importance of our ground combat forces. During the course of the war they declined in

proportionate size and relative importance as com-
pared with our air forces. At the same time this Army,
properly so called, shared, as has been noted, in an
unprecedented growth of services, accompanied by an
apparently uncontrollable proliferation of "overhead"
in the form of huge and complicated headquarters.

Since the war there has been no increase of relative
emphasis on the combat mission of the Army, and this
mission is unlikely to regain its former importance in
our system of making war unless the United States
should be threatened with invasion. In consonance
with this tendency the Air Force has become inde-
pendent; the War Department has become the Department of the Army; and the successor to the Secretary of War, shorn of his control of the air forces, is
now a Secretary of the Army, without a seat in the
President's Cabinet.

Yet the Army, as now constituted, has a place and
prestige in our system of defense that gives it enormous
weight and importance. And it has a more numerous,
complex, and imposing superstructure of staff and
command than ever before in its history. This superstructure and the chain of command are complicated
by a maze of liaison, committees, management experts,
and joint boards. These are regarded with great un-
easiness and concern by officers bred and schooled in
the conviction that the two basic laws of military dis-
cipline and effectiveness are that command is single
and responsibility is indivisible. Recently I heard one
of them exclaim bitterly: "If they would give us back
the Army, we would be all right!" That wish seems as

likely to be fulfilled as the cry of the cavalryman: "If they would only give me back my horse!"

An explanation of their bewilderment and concern, and of the apparently anomalous position of the Army, seems to lie in the fact, not yet fully recognized, that the primary mission of the Army under our present system is, quantitatively speaking, no longer ground combat, but administration. This displacement of basic function, as has been observed in the foregoing survey, was taking place rapidly during World War II. It began with the fact that ground combat in that war required mechanical paraphernalia, a profusion of supplies, logistical services, and therefore administration, on a scale never previously approached. But this was not all. The Army was the only instrument of our Government that had an organization capable of effecting the orderly assembly, movement, and distribution of great masses of men and materiel over great distances. It excelled in administration. Consequently, in addition to its combat mission, it was charged with the task of administering military Lend-Lease to our Allies, supplying the civilian populations of the territories occupied by Allied forces, and responsibility not only for military government but for the administration of civil affairs in areas occupied by the forces of the United States. Commanders like General Mc-Nair who were single-minded in their belief that the overriding mission of the Army was to fight and that all other missions were "frills," and who therefore tried to keep its organizations lean and simple, fought a losing battle.

Since 1945 the administrative responsibilities of the

Army have been extended still further. It not only does the housekeeping for its own establishment, builds its own bases, and invents, develops, procures, and moves its own munitions and supplies, but, as agent of the Department of Defense, it now shares largely in the performance of these services for the Navy, the Marines, and the Air Force. In the case of the Marines, the Army and Navy perform these services to such an extent that the Marines are in the position that the Army once shared with them of being able to concentrate their thought and training on a single function: ground combat. The role of the Army in the realm of administration reached a new degree of magnitude and national importance when the Army was charged with the administration of a whole tri-service and multi-national war—the war in Korea.

The administrative proficiency of the Army is signalized by the eagerness with which the business world has taken over the Army's wartime leaders to manage big business. But the Army takes only incidental pride in administrative proficiency. Its pride is still rooted in battle proficiency, and many of its leaders are bewildered and confused and feel ill at ease in an Army equipped with the elaborate, and often semicivilian, coordinations and controls that the complexity and variety of its new tasks have produced. The irony of the situation is that the Army's brilliant successes in large-scale administration that contributed to its present constitution and estate may well have depended, very largely, on the principles that "command is single" and "responsibility is indivisible." The problem of preserving these principles in an organization whose mission is no longer simple has not yet been solved, either by the Army, or by American public administration, or, for that matter, by big business. Just as serious, or even more serious, in this period of national danger, may be the problem of maintaining a corps of Army officers and troops with the morale and concentration of purpose of the officers who trained and commanded our Army Ground Forces in World War II.